# Feeling Some Type Of Way

## By Sodo Austin

Foreword by Lonnie D. Perkins

Cadmus Publishing
CadmusPublishing.com

# FEELING SOME TYPE OF WAY

Manufactured in the United States of America. Copyright 2025 by Sodo Austin. All rights reserved. No part of this book may be reproduced in any form, audio, digital, or in print, except excerpts by reviewers, without written permission from the copyright holder or Cadmus Publishing LLC.

DISCLAIMER:
 The thoughts, opinions, and expressions herein are those of the author and do not reflect those of Cadmus Publishing LLC. Any similarities to actual events or people are purely coincidental. Names and distinguishing characteristics may have been changed to preserve the identities of any individuals. Published by Cadmus Publishing LLC. P. O. Box 8664. Haledon, NJ 07538

Web: Cadmuspublishing.com
Web: Booksbyprisoners.com
Web: MusicbyPrisoners.com
Facebook.com/Cadmuspublishing
Business email: admin@cadmuspublishing.com
Author email: info@cadmuspublishing.com
Phone: 360.565.6459

ISBN# 978-1-63751-551-8
Library of Congress Control Number: 2025951416
 Book Catalog Info Categories:
   African American/Urban Life

Cadmus Publishing
CadmusPublishing.com

# Acknowledgements

First & Foremost, I would like to Acknowledge the most high, most merciful, for continuing to give me the gift of writing & sharing my ability. Secondly, I want to Acknowledge my Brody "KD" (Donovan, Haley) for supporting & believing in the push that is BitterChild, Sodo, Austin, & Bitter 2 Better Foundation, one bitter child one nation! I would like to Acknowledge my love life & wife Cynthia Ortega, for her love & support, love you much bay. I would also like to Acknowledge my moms & pops Dorothy & Tony, I appreciate your love & support. I would also like to Acknowledge my Aunt Marty Lou, love you always & my uncle Johnny (R.I.P.), love you infinity. I would like to Acknowledge Six, September, for playing a part in this journey & supporting the push from the beginning. I would like to Acknowledge my young man's & nem K'vion Cruz, tear it off! I would also like to Acknowledge my daughter Christina Odessa & her lil people. Love Always, pops.

FEELING SOME TYPE OF WAY—SODO AUSTIN

# FORWARD: "Rerun"

By Lonnie D. Perkins

When Sodo asked me to write the forward for this work, Feeling Some Type Of Way, it automatically welcomed me to vent about a lot of things that rub me the wrong way!

The #1 thing that's high on the list are those individuals (you know who you are) who think they are slicker than snot and can sell ice to an Eskimo! Little do they know that I can see them coming 4 miles away with their watered down drag, thinking that they popping something original, not knowing the game has been done to death, or as I'm fond of saying, "It's a rerun just like they are!!!"

You know how when you run across someone whose mannerism is similar to a person you've met before (usually not leaving a good impression) and you say in your mind, "I know your kind?" Well, these present days I'm pretty swift in my level of thinking and can analyze game within a few words, add body language to the equation and I will stereotype someone to the tee and be on point with it more times than not!

Now let me keep it clean off the dribble. I can be vindictive and hold a serious grudge, especially to those whom I've succumbed to their drag before (fool me once, shame on them). Shame me twice and we'll have a situation! Hell, if the kid who cheated me in marbles back in 1972 cross paths with me today, I'll have something to say cause I'm just wired that way. (Really though...)

But I digress, because I feel some kind of way about bullshit people and the things they do, 'cause after all "Game is only good as long as you

## FEELING SOME TYPE OF WAY—SODO AUSTIN

don't get caught!" And depending on the level of the transgression, may the Good Lord bless you and the Undertaker dress you. (Amen)

One of the shadiest men that I've ever known was called Scandalous Black (RIP).

He was an older East Side dude out of Los Angeles who ran around the prison system doing every lowdown dirty trick in the book to get over on people back in the days when nonsense got you an extra belly button (stabbed). Something he was no stranger to in prison on several occasions, but he didn't care as long as he got high on people he should tell them that we were related, thinking he would get a pass when he burned them for something, usually dope. So when they would hit me up about "Is he my cousin?" I automatically knew that he did some low shit, and my reply was always the same: "Put some iron in his diet" (stab him)...

I learned a lot from watching Scandalous Black and actually would give him stuff when he came popping his drag, thinking he had talked up on something, but anything I gave him I didn't expect to get paid in money for. Instead I got paid by learning what game to watch for, because like I said, I respect game, but if I catch you I'm going to feel some type of way!

Word is, someone gave Scandalous Black a hot shot (spiked dope) that he injected and it killed him. So the moral of the story is: "Making people feel some kind of way can be a health hazard and, kids, don't play with matches!!!"

Introduction

# FEELING SOME TYPE OF WAY—SODO AUSTIN

Feeling Some Type Of Way is basically my having strong feelings and emotions towards and about issues I deem worthy of speaking on, as I'd done with Yard Life (Expose - Real Life Inside of Prison). Yes, I get emo and work with feelings as we all do about things around us and in traffic (the streets) as a whole. However, they'll always be relevant and will be relevant based on the many different mindsets and actions we're subjected to. Being out there. Being exposed to the things we're exposed to and experiencing the things that come along with those exposures (SMH). All while being mindful of the fact that we're continuing to have these experiences and exposures, yet expecting different results. But shit, I can still vent to the world and share my exposures and experiences as I experienced then and were exposed to them. I guess though too I'm just adamant about young homie getting his Chucks (Chuck Taylors) laced up. Giving him that exposure and knowledge to the elements that exist around him and how, for the most part, a lot of things aren't what they seem or appear to be, and things are constantly evolving and not in a good way. In some instances the facts are thee same generally, though they change with the times. Faces change and shenanigans change but never the commodities. More ""flags on the play," more "ball playing" and more "no fly zones." As always I'll continue to call a ball a ball and a strike a strike when it comes to circumstances dictating the courses in life that we take. My same lens, my same focus, reality! The view never changes. A photo shop couldn't change it, based on its survival value, and it not just being one of those things that give value to survival. One thing you'll continue to find is you're constantly learning and having to reset and adjust.

## FEELING SOME TYPE OF WAY—SODO AUSTIN

You're adjusting b'cuz shit just got more complexed, just went another level of trickery, crookedness, sideways and shenanigan.

Some things you can come back from, some you can't. Hopefully, you can, though, depending on the situation or whether or not it's just one of those lessons learned moments and you can't keep it moving, chalking it up to a life lesson. It's all in what you experience and are exposed to, by who and what manner it came. The how, could be the change that changes the whole dynamic in the lesson which in essence can affect your movements moving forward. One thing's for certain, there's a lesson to be learned. Now, whether you choose to take heed to it or not is on you. I'm just doing what I feel is my due diligence.

My overstanding is hopefully where your adjustment comes in route. overstanding that everything does come in full circle. Just in a different form, which is the reality and life as we come to know it to be. Shit can also come at you and time isn't of the essence. You can't prepare for it. B'cuz there's this thing called "Shit happens unexpectedly," especially dealing with the elements we're dealing with, dealing with these unpredictable dudes, their emo, the wrong type of emo, though, factoring in the gang drugs (meth, heroin, PCP and opioids) and alcohol, adding the worst case of the "Fuck its!" Adding even more unpredictability and shenanigans in the field of play, that much more drama and bullshit.

It's already foul, cruel, evil, self serving and twisted, with little to no morals, values or loyalty. Still considering the other elements of the streets that's lurking around every corner like a shadow niggah (someone who's

## FEELING SOME TYPE OF WAY—SODO AUSTIN

not trying to be seen during daylight hours). Off the dribble, a better overstanding of the life and mentality, as well as a better overstanding of the potential exposures and experiences that's going to more than likely rear up their head based on.

I guess this concludes the "Intro," but in any event stay focused, stay mindful and pay attention as you're moving about in your lane, every lane isn't a passing one...

Sanity is screwed up/homie deaded in vain/burn the water in the cut/mashin against the grain/niggah know the game though/niggah switch the lane/snitches and bustahs remain bussin/can't even aim straight/conversation is strange/moves is kind of hasty/picture the 2 faces/bots in the grave wit 'em/codes is bein bent/still hard to trust niggahs/wings bein clipped/on sight wit the rush niggah/viewin any critics/yeah you can duck wit 'em/still talkin shit/pressure bust pipes/it's yard life niggah/how deep is yo sess pool?/needles being moved too/misled troopin/so one still catchin blues so/fuck what the truth is/niggah no proof/way dirty wit his pitch so/claim is unglued so/homie not cool/what?/lost in his fame yup/lame niggahs do/but say that he gang-gang/isms lay rooted/how can I blame you?/just be you/but keep watchin Judas/Autobots too/wrong kind of famous/sparks come through/that's where the hate is/just bein truthful/niggah round two/my visuals yo hang up/drawn from conclusions...

## FEELING SOME TYPE OF WAY—SODO AUSTIN

CONTENTS

Acknowledgements

Forward: "Rerun" by Lonnie D. Perkins

Introduction

N.I.G.G.A.H. (Poem)

Thoughts

Chapters

(1) You Ain't Shit

(2) A Snitch Anywhere Is A Threat To Real Niggahs Everywhere

(3) Yard Life

(4) Come To The Turf

(5) Rabbs Change Shit

(6) Going Against The Grain

Spoken: "In The City Niggah"

(7) What You Signed Up For

(8) Somebody Have To Learn The Hard Way

(9) G Homie

(10) It Get Real

(11) Loyalty

(12) Ground Work

Spoken: "I'm A Mover"

## FEELING SOME TYPE OF WAY—SODO AUSTIN

Outroduction

Death is imminent/running in them streets/on the wrong side of the barrel/holes got you breezy/wrong corner to post on/fuckin wit the east/niggah long gone/shook and can't sleep/situation is dead wrong/niggahs still beefin/blocks is still zoned/tires is still screechin/drama is full blown/it's the same damn song/lost to the keepers/politicals drove it/faces is never shown/thrown/homies done turned foes/shadows still creepin/sleep til we recognotice the life of a dying breed/ties forever broken/T.I.C./yeah niggah loc shit/wit a press on the street/yeah where that smoke be/bitches think I'm dope/I rep where I live/and I'm sticky like a post-it/I speak to my ghost niggahs/walk a burned bridge/many bitches ghosted/love six kids/sherm took focus/took it to the head/chase rabbs til I'm dead/I'm always on the edge/always flies in my web/so...I fuck wit les bitches/secrets always kept/many snakes in the trenches/sit behind a tint/yeah bear witness/cool on niggahs shit/stay swingin fo the fences/so...you can eat a dick/and still bang crip...

# FEELING SOME TYPE OF WAY—SODO AUSTIN

Contents:

[The Table of Contents in Feeling Some Type Of Way, from the Introduction to the Outroduction were strategically titled and placed, for all intended purposes, the method to my bitterology...]

# FEELING SOME TYPE OF WAY—SODO AUSTIN

N.I.G.G.A.H. (Poem)

He's my folks, she's my relly, those my homies and that's my family. Hello my brothah, good day my sistah, to all my loved ones and to you my niggah...

My niggahs come in all of its ethnicities, accents and all sizes, languages, cultures, colors and disguises, we are educated, motivated, most creative and discriminated against...

Sophisticated, underpaid and underestimated, from Thomas L. Jennings to Dr. Daniel Hale Williams, my niggahs are noble, inspiring, captivating, intellectual, genuine and authentic, like John F. Kennedy, Juliette Morgan and Bill Clinton...

The definition of attitude, some wild, some rude, some silent, just like you. Made of flesh and blood, red and blue, exceptionally falling short, but acceptable, thirsty for success, only one place left to go, hell was the test...

N.I.G.G.E.R., a phrase created from the streets to detain, a word used to overpower a single race, used to try an separate what God set in place. N.I.G.G.A.H., a phrase created from the streets to detain the effect of segregation in the world without peace...

Word envisioned by a younger generation, waiting to be set free, havoc on a nation, let it not be forgotten, now deaded and rotten, children slaughtered, mamas raped, niggahs lynched and so to pick cotton...

Priceless slaves fighting to ride in the front of the bus, to drink from the same fountain as us, for the same education or at least the correct books, unable to wear a hoodie or enjoy your drink, pull out a wallet in the middle of the street...

## FEELING SOME TYPE OF WAY—SODO AUSTIN

Frowned upon when loving another complexion and even with death upon this plantation. We learned a lesson, no sense of compassion or direction. N.I.G.G.E.R. was a woman, now just a scar cutting the ropes, balls and chain, birth by the Lord, assorted only by gender and names... N.I.G.G.A.H., a word used at your own risk, your own consent. Not a reminder of where we are from but where we were sent, he's my folks, she's my relly, those my homies and that's my family. Hello my brotah, good day my sistah, to all my loved ones and to you my niggah... A word only has meaning when taken to heart, lifting one up, or tearing thousands apart.

# FEELING SOME TYPE OF WAY—SODO AUSTIN

Thoughts:
The reality of this street shit cause niggahs to pause, fallin short of the cautions, wonder how they press play, conversations be cross talking, illuminated the situation...
Wounds hittin targets, jail birds caged, shadow niggahs sparkin, got to play the shade, niggahs friendships is staged, got to change the lane up, slam on the brakes, left look right look, the streets been dangerous...
Niggahs on the take, you Autobots is janky, I've been around 'em from the gate, lines are never straight though, you can see it in my face, gaze cuttin like a razor, it's a weary demonstration...
The streets are far from what they used to be, especially from the era I grew up in, which was the 80s, whole different ball game and field of play. Same principles but different elements, with a lot more unpredictability that lies and lurks around a corner, the dangers that lurk. Mind you, you're dealing with all of the different personalities, and picture these personalities on the "gang drugs," uppers and downers combined with the "drank" (alcohol). It's bringing different energy and a whole different element to the table and just that much more unpredictability and shenanigans (SMH). You're not only dealing with the unpredictability of the streets, but the unpredictability of the individuals in the streets, we're surrounded by on a daily, dudes we surround ourselves with.
You always have to be mindful of who you surround yourself with, bitches included, they're never exempt from the unpredictabilities, dangers, or shenanigans that lurks and lies in the streets. Day one of jumping off the

# FEELING SOME TYPE OF WAY—SODO AUSTIN

porch. "Cube" (Ice Cube) said it best, never trust a big ass and a smile. It's levels to this street shit, beyond just the fact of it being a cold cold world we live in. It's unforgiving, it's cancel culture, it's cruel, uncaring, devious, unloyal, it's untrustworthy and it doesn't give a mad fuck about a niggah like you or me. It's even colder today. More unforgiving, more crueler, more uncaring and more devious, it's quicker to be cancelled out, even more unloyalty and untrustworthiness. The streets of today could really give less than three hot fucks about a niggah, what he represents, where he's from, what he knows or who he's related to, being out there in them and living that life, let alone the breath he breathes.

Your life has no value and caries no weight. You're either a "means" or "a means to an end," which you'll come to overstand and realize when that energy is forced to reveal itself, exposing that reality that was so deeply tucked in the shadows, showing you just how much you were really loved, respected, cared about, valued or appreciated in that realm. The realm of relationships, bonds, ties and connections as they pertain to the streets and in them. It's crucial in the "field" (streets) and gets really real, nothing for the most part is as it seems, when it comes to the daily interactions and movements. That in which we see, yet we still tend to brush shit off or be dismissive of it, being blinded by the false senses of security, the intake of mind altering substances, both drugs and drank, that's taking our inability to be focused, therefore allowing that reality and testament that exists to be shielded. What reality and testament? The fakeness, the disloyalty and the flag on the play.

## FEELING SOME TYPE OF WAY—SODO AUSTIN

It's far too easy, I mean easy as fuck to get caught up in them. Far too easy to become a victim of them. Death is imminent and catching a bunch of time is imminent, it's designed that way when you're out there in that life and being about that life. There's no middle ground when you choose to "press play" (act or be involved) you're choosing all that comes with it, the rhythm, the blues, it's raw and uncut when you're hanging, banging or slanging and it's always one way to do shit and that's the right way. There's only 2 outcomes that's going to happen and will happen, you're deaded or you're locked up with a gang of time, period, point blank. It's cut and dry, no bars held, there's no getting around it. You're going to find yourself on an emotional roller coaster, find yourself shedding more than a few tears. You're going to find yourself shook up, traumatized, paranoid and feeling some type of way about a lot of different shit, most definitely find yourself feeling betrayed.

You'll find anger clouding and love blinding, but unswayed from how you're feeling about a situation. You're going to find yourself coming to learn, overstand and know dudes are not going to be who they say they are and painted their self to be. Finding out that the whole time it was an illusion of truth to wear that mask of deception well, bitches too! What they say they were about. You're going to find out just how loyal a muthah fuckah is to you and what common interests y'all share. You're going to be relationship tested and battle tested, coming to find yourself having respect for the streets with a greater respect for them, based on coming to learn how and overstand that they don't give a flying fuck about you and

## FEELING SOME TYPE OF WAY—SODO AUSTIN

will have you. Your awareness will be acknowledged off the dribble. Who you are, what you think you're about, what you think you're with, who your folks are or who you run with don't mean shit to the streets. Don't none of that carry weight. Do the wrong thing, be caught in a compromising position or do something, and see just how much that shit weigh or mean. It holds none and don't mean shit, it is what it is. You're just another dude in the streets and are expendable basically. You'll be had just as quick as the next niggah and whoever you have with you, fucking with you, ducking with you! One thing I know for certain, death and jail doesn't discriminate or is biased. The streets don't discriminate or have "biases" when it comes to being in the life. Shit being "Mickey" or going "Mickey" is inevitable! That's the energy and how the ball bounces. That's me calling a ball a ball and a strike a strike.

Being in the field doing and being you, shit comes with consequences and it can cost more than you're willing to pay. Just as you think you have shit figured out or individuals, you're hit with another twist and turn that presents itself in a way a dude would've never saw coming. It was under the radar. Believe half of what you hear and half of what you see. It's said somewhere, and you see what you see. You don't need an Autobot to convince you of a reality. On some win, lose or draw type shit, me personally "Feeling Some Type Of Way" has me saying what it is I'm saying. How I'm saying it and to the extent and depth is due to the emotions and feelings evoked within me, deriving from a constant and steady view of my seeing dudes caught up and being twisted by different variables that come into play.

# FEELING SOME TYPE OF WAY—SODO AUSTIN

In the ways of the "set" and in the ways of the street, just seeing the outcome of "play" being "pressed," seeing the outcomes being what they are and have been and not looking good for the home team. Seeing how dudes get ran up out of the set from being voted off the island and being banished. Seeing how dudes take their batteries out of their backs. Seeing how dudes are politiced and ball played on them. Seeing how Autobots play a role in a lot of dudes' demise, being "Mickey" (SMH). Seeing how dudes in general get fucked over being in the game or in the life and playing it half-assed. Seeing a dude finding out it wasn't all that it was cracked up to be, ending up on the wrong end of the barrel. "BLOOOM!!!!" You know what else is a trip and is "Mickey" will also be a trip and "Mickey" is how you'll find out all types of shit about homies and dudes you know and knew to be straight (solid) or for the most part thought was straight, or led to believe was straight, only to have a dude be disappointed, let down and feeling some type of way, coming to learn otherwise.

Coming to learn dude was a scumbag, Mickey, or done snitched (SMH), snitch on a homie or on the next niggah back in the "day...day." Yeah, a dirty little secret only a few dudes from the set know about and helped keep concealed from going "viral" (SMH), be it a younger homie, a big homie, or a "G" homie. And from how they were getting down back then, it kind of explains the issues in retrospect certain "G" homies were having with one another, feeling some type of way about each other over the years. Then seeing how when certain G's would come around and how other ones would do it moving, put some validity to it. Looking back on it

## FEELING SOME TYPE OF WAY—SODO AUSTIN

now and keying in on certain situations and conversations, and how homies were pushing (moving). It explains certain actions, movements being made and how homies were being got at verbally and accepting it. Yeah, I know what you did last summer type shit, you have no room to talk back or be in your feelings! Without having to verbalize it, niggahs give that "You know what's up" look. That "Go ahead trip, I'll put you out there" (expose whatever dirt's being canceled). It also explains why certain dudes weren't having or getting that respect you felt they should've been, based on their activities and representation.

Not just from homies, but "G" homies cut from that same cloth. Dudes are very respectful to energy and movements, and will follow suit, especially younger homies. If they see "G" homies or older homies not fucking with homies of their generation and treating them a certain way with the same energy and movements, it explains it and gives it perspective. And due to who these dudes are, it's like whoa...him! I couldn't believe my ears, as far as what they were hearing, but coming from who it was coming from it was credible (SMH).

B'cuz of the homie it's coming from and came from, isn't known for the scandalous shit, shenanigans, Autobotism, or known to partake in dirty politics and being a dirty politician. Nor is he the type to put jackets on dudes that don't deserve to wear them, if it's not true or have validity. Based on him knowing and respecting the seriousness of an accusation and how it'll go viral and travel, how crooked it'll go quick, fast and in a hurry, no doubt it's going to be a "Mickey" situation. At the end of the day,

## FEELING SOME TYPE OF WAY—SODO AUSTIN

it's not him or his demo (demonstration) or what he's about. Then like, I stressed seeing what I've observed and then hearing something thereafter, years later it kind of fit and made sense as to dudes' characters, you just never know. You'll find a lot of that, finding out dudes aren't who they put themselves out there to be, a straight "Gilligan" and a "vermin."

Dudes faked the get down and been faking the get down all along, yet masquerading around like they're built a certain way and move a certain way when that ain't the case and is basically an illusion of the worst kind. But that's "G" niggahs dirty lil secrets they have with their collective and amongst themselves, that's younger homies and "BG's" lil dirty secrets they have within their collective and amongst themselves, only certain dudes are privy to that info. It always manage to find itself coming out, bit by bit. These are the type of dudes and homies, though, dudes are fucking with and looking up to and calling "Big Homie" (SMH). Snitch niggahs and niggahs condoning it, b'cuz these same niggahs are allowed to be in the set and allowed to function with these homies, knowing their demo and their past.

It's just crazy to a dude, but I've learned to expect the unexpected and see shit for what and as it is, nothing more and nothing less. But that's just what it is and my thing is this, and as it's been, due to my being a firm believer in the sentiment: "A snitch anywhere is a threat to real niggahs everywhere." How can he not be? Riddle me that! So do overstand, it's a lot of bullshit being condoned and being orchestrated in the "set" and in the streets as a whole, being navigated through the maze. You're getting to find yourself not living safe, therefore living dangerous. Be vigilant and

## FEELING SOME TYPE OF WAY—SODO AUSTIN

proactive in your push and always strive to be a real niggah, as only you can be. Don't worry about the next niggah on some Autobot shit, on some fake shit or on some buster ass shit he's on. That's not supposed to reflect you or how you're pushing. You be the dude that's keeping it a "hunnid" and pushing your push vigilantly. You be that dude mindful of all that is and of all that could be. Being a dude never taking being above ground for granted, b'cuz as soon as you do you will find yourself below that muthah fuckah, being mourned, cried over and with niggahs wearing white T's with your face on them, on some rest in peace type shit and your homies being pallbearers at your funeral. On that note, my niggah, I'm going to leave you with this. It's not so much of what you do but how you do what you do.

If you stand for right and support only that which is right, keeping it solid and a hunnid, and that's what you're "demonstrating," you'll be alright. Have a greater respect for your push and get down, respect it for what it is and how you're pushing it. Always be mindful too of what unpredictabilities that's a constant and a constant lurk like a shadow niggah! As with the "evil" witness lurking, don't be a victim to the ways and of the ways of the set or to the ways, and of the ways of the streets, fucking with your surroundings, the dudes and bitches you fuck with. Don't be defined or let your get down and push be defined.

Regardless of the tale, the streets gon speak on it...evidently compelling, that's the muthah fuckin streets fo yah. The shit a niggah faced with on a day to day and what a niggah make of it, what a niggah make of it...

# Chapter 1

## "You Ain't Shit"

For those that want to know, not only how a bitch, baby mama, or wife can do time with a niggah, but his homies or his people as well, loyalty...straight up! Notice, I didn't use the word "family" but rather his "people," for the simple fact "family" is just merely a word. It means nothing, the word doesn't automatically make you family, loyalty does. Otherwise, you're just related by blood. As for "loyalty," it's a word that a lot of muthah fuckahs have no comprehension of. That shit is really foreign to them. As for her (bitch, baby mama, wife), if she's with the right niggah, I guess. I think that's giving her too much credit b'cuz for the most part I don't think that even matters when it's not in her to do. I don't care how much she claimed to have loved or cared about you, get locked up and see how quick her energy changes up. You'll most definitely get that reality check, exposing just what it was. But it took for you to get locked up to see the reality of what you thought was there, which apparently meant nothing. You know what, you wouldn't have known it otherwise.

It took a real situation to expose the reality. Situations or circumstances have a tendency to expose shit for what and as they are. At the end of the day, we know the type of "bitch, homie" or blood relative we have, so it really shouldn't come as a shock when we see they aren't who we thought they were. With her, though, you see how it came as second nature to dismiss the relationship as if it never existed (SMH).

# FEELING SOME TYPE OF WAY—SODO AUSTIN

Don't get me wrong, the same can be said for homies or relatives, thus creating that pessimistic spin on the way we see them. The cold thing about it, they're not real enough, not even a little bit to let a niggah know what the deal is, yet claim to be real. The pill would be a lot easier to swallow if only they kept it a hunnid. How can a niggah not respect it?

Nah, they rather horseplay, lie and play games, creating hostility and drama when it didn't have to be, which was a premeditated choice and conscious decision on their part. The horseplay, lies and games could've been avoided, yet they chose to ride with them instead of letting real things and real situations take their course. The thing is, we already know you're going to do and be you (I'm talking to her). To expect anything else is a mis-overstanding. It's a part of the dynamic of us no longer having or being a presence.

The energy is expected to shift. It's just what it is. But even with that, it shouldn't stop them from doing us (niggahs locked up) and playing a position. A niggah give a fuck about some "dick and pussy" shit (her having sex), that's ill-relavant, nor is it a concern or issue. A niggah locked up, and more than likely will be for a cool minute (long time), do what you do (live your life as only you do). Though they're doing and being them, it apparently doesn't stop them from playing a position or wanting to, when it shouldn't. I guess it's just easier to move on and put distance between the situation without a heads up. It's just crazy to me, how easy it is for them to remove themselves from the equation without hesitation

## FEELING SOME TYPE OF WAY—SODO AUSTIN

(SMH). Personally, I rather for her to be straight up, like look, "I'm not trying to do this jail shit. It's not me."

That's what I love and respected the most about McNeal (one of my side chicks), she knew my lifestyle, she knew I was jail bound, I'm selling dope, jacking, not to mention gang-banging, so the risk was high. She knew it and I knew it, "Bluey Bluey" was inevitable. She told me straight up, "You know how you're living and the chances you're taking, if you go to jail, I'm gone." She didn't take away my choices in regards to giving me the choice to bounce, knowing her position or accepting her position for what and as it was and continuing to fuck with her. Which I did based on I knew the deal and accepted it. Turned out she hung around briefly, and we went our way on good terms.

I can accept and respect shit for what and as it is, as long as I know the deal, especially under these circumstances (being locked up) due to overstanding the limitations and the nature of the maze. I rather, though, she being on the other end come correct than to be horseplaying. Therefore, I'm not in my "F and E's" (feelings and emotions) about the situation (situation-ship) and we're still on cool terms and she's not a bunch of scandalous ass bitches when she does it moving (leave). I call it "preventative maintenance" if it's a thing, so that down the line if she wants to pull back up (come back) it's good b'cuz we didn't leave on a bad note. That's only initially her leaving like fresh off a dude getting the time. It applies only to him getting a lot of it (15+ years all the way to life). I feel a dude can do at least a "ten piece" (10 years) and solo if need be. I

## FEELING SOME TYPE OF WAY—SODO AUSTIN

mean, shit, we can do it all solo if it came to that, especially not having a choice but to do it solo. Who, though, wouldn't mind having that support system and energy? They're giving us that energy we need to help ease the journey, not just the financial energy but the mental, emotional and physical energy as well, but as only they can. Even if they can't help you with the financial energy, they could still pull up and be involved, having a presence, it didn't take much. Hit a dude with a few lines on paper or send captured moments (pictures) every now and then. If that's the only way you feel you can be involved, let a dude know he's at least thought about. He can respect and accept the doing what you can as only you can. It's you playing your position. Its not so much as about what you can provide financially, though it helps. Don't let that be the reason, though, you don't pull up feeling if you can't slide no financial energy, you have nothing to contribute.

Don't get it wrong, there are dudes who may feel that way, but you can't put everyone in that same box. Everyone locked up aren't on that. Don't use that as a way out. On the flip side of that, it's overstood everyone isn't in a position financially to assist and are aware of the struggles out there in everyday life, just trying to survive. That's never overlooked, forgotten or lost in translation. Just checking all the way out, though, what part of the game is that? The shit that kills me, though, is when she come to her realization in depth, not giving shit much thought at first and being quick to agree to some shit as far as what it entails, as a whole, as to the role and position. The roll and position she really intended on playing.

## FEELING SOME TYPE OF WAY—SODO AUSTIN

Then when it's thought out thoroughly and the realization do set in, it's like, hold up. Now she doesn't want to continue being a presence or having one. If the "fall off" is inevitable she'll start gradually making her exit. First the mail slows down from twice a week to once a week, then to every other week, then to once a month. The "fall off" is for real! Now you can't catch her on the phone and when you do the conversation is short and dry as fuck (she's really not trying to talk, but forcing herself to entertain the conversation).

From that to not catching her dusty ass for days at a time. She starts lying to you about small shit, the shenanigans and noise are in full effect, all gas. Then you stop hearing from her altogether and no longer able to even call. Yeah, she bounced that ass (SMH), which means she got herself a "situationship," feeling she has to separate herself so she can do and be her without having to feel some type of way about it. Suffering from that case of "can't chew bubble gum and walk at the same time syndrome." Usually, the telltale signs are there, her energy is a dead give away. I personally feel the give away was there from the "get-go," she just didn't know how to approach the situation, not wanting to have you up in your "F and E's," but the reality is she made the situation that much worse when it didn't have to be a situation at all. For me, my overstanding is never zero. If you tell me this isn't what you're trying to do, "Ain't that's wassup!" I can respect the fact you were a woman about the situation and not a girl, feeling the need to play the game of going through the motions, until you decided to hit the exit ramp.

## FEELING SOME TYPE OF WAY—SODO AUSTIN

I can respect you being real with yourself first and foremost, and allowing yourself to be real with me. Anything outside of that, though, you ain't shit! The quicker you accept it the quicker you'll get over it! So they say. How can you really get over being buried mentally, emotionally and physically by those that claim to have your back and claim to have love for you without having resentment towards them? These same individuals that called you family, homie, baby daddy, husband or your girl. Yet you can't pick up the phone and log in (call them). Yet you can't send a visiting form and get a visit. Yet you can't put a canteen slip in and go to canteen. Yet you can't send a package form and get a package. Yet they can't take a few minutes out of their day to day to "tap in" with a few dots and dashes on paper, a few lines, or send a few captured moments.

But they're family, they're the homie, baby mama, wifey or your girl. Negative breeds negative! Yet you wonder why a niggah calling you "bullshit" or saying, "You ain't shit!" Trials and actions have a way of forcing you to reevaluate and rethink relationships, coming to the realization that we were only believing in images and seeing masks which you're forced to take notice of, sitting in the cell day after day whether it's on the "mainline" or in the "sandbox" doing a SHU term. Things seem to become clear and come more into focus as each day passes, having to reflect and come to grip with reality in this maze.

To you the relationship or "situationship" meant something and held value to the extent you felt confident of your place in their space, only to be hit with that harsh reality check, it meant nothing. The direction change is inevitable, "Brody" (Bro). Yeah, they wanted the rhythm, but not the blues. What we face transforms us and have us in our "F and E's" from frustration and feeling betrayed. Like, I can't believe this bitch! I can't believe this niggah! I can't believe this shit! This is the mindset and general consensus. The more time that lapses without contact or communication of any kind, the more distance is put in between you and the situation to the point of no recovery, it's too far gone, then it's to the point of the fuck its! Now it's like I'm over it, and you, K.T.S.E.! What you thought, though? At some point the trajectory in terms of attitude was bound to change.

    I know for me, there's no pulling back up on me, I'm straighter than Indian hair! Like my niggahs from Babyz (Baby Insane Gang). Like, we're going to reset the go button. No bueno! That ship has sailed 20 years ago. There's nothing for us to reset on or talk about, nor is there a reason, any reason, for us to have a relationship or attempt to build one. What would be the reason? We ain't been talking, we ain't having a relationship! I've been in prison for the past 20 years. Where have you been? Not fucking with me! I ain't heard a peep. The question is, why would I want to be? Don't need you, ain't ever needed you, been cool without you! And as long as it's been, I don't even know you and at this point in the game, don't want to know you. So it's really not a loss to me not having you in my space. There's no emotional or mental attachment, definitely no love!

    Your actions towards me showed me the depth of how and what you felt. However, the plus is, I can stress you've made me a much stronger and deeper person mentally and gauging me to process complex movements and thoughts, also teaching me to not settle for anything less than the standards I have! It could've all been so simple. I don't mind the scars and bruises. I'm just not feeling the stories they tell. I'm looking at those who counted "Tic" out, buried me and said fuck me. Look at me now, though! It's still "Bitter Child," can't stop. Won't stop. Don't stop! Never letting a hard time or difficult struggle humble me, get a bar!

When push comes to shove, I don't need your fake love, friendship, or loyalty, understanding there are no true allies, just interest outside of Moms and my Aunt Marty Lou. I thought I had an ally in my Cuzzo Nip, but like everyone else his energy came with conditions or just wasn't there. His interaction with me was, to an extent, so like everyone else that was temporarily in my space, I had to fall back and give him his space and give him distance. However, I'll always appreciate what he's done, even if it wasn't genuinely done. Did he have to assist me where he had? Not at all. So for that, I appreciate him nevertheless, based on that. When it's all said and done, though, he's no different than everyone else, which I realized, based on his energy towards shit that didn't matter versus the shit that did. I get it and overstand it, though, for what and as it is. I'm not even mad at him. He done more than most were willing to do or have done, outside of my Mama and Aunt Marty Lou and Unc Johnny, which is his mama and his step pops (RIP), my God Bro Darren, the homie Mike Mosley aka Dirty Mike and a female named Darla I met in the early 90's who's pulled up on me with energy on a few occasions.

# FEELING SOME TYPE OF WAY—SODO AUSTIN

Moms, though, my Aunt and my Unc, have always been there day one! Baby mamas, no bueno! Period. At no time have any of my baby mamas ever pulled up on me while I've been doing time and tried to holler at me in no capacity. It was as if we've never existed or have been in a situationship or have kids. In all reality, I knew the type I was breeding with and dealing with off the dribble, based on how we met a where we met. Bitches with no loyalty, value, morals or sense of self or self-respect. And at no time had I been locked up past or present had any of them let me communicate with my kids or have anything to do with them. Never brought them to see me, never sent captured moments, never wrote! (Never helped to write me, never encouraged it, never wrote themselves to let me know what was going on with them) But...what they did do was get in the next situationship and had the kids calling the next niggah daddy (SMH).

To this day, I have no relationship with any of my kids, due in part b'cuz of the lack of communication and lack of encouragement to communicate with me while they were kids, to no fault of their own, I'll give them that. I'll admit and can admit, I was locked up for the better part of their lives, being in and out of jail. So, I play a role in that myself, based on my not being there with them or for them. However, it didn't have to end there. OK, I was locked up, still locked up now. But like me, knowing them, my "BM's" knew me, knew my lifestyle and how I was living life. So the threat of me going to jail or being killed was always at the forefront, being a street niggah in the streets and a jail niggah, that's just what's going on with me. So basically, since I went to jail or came to

## FEELING SOME TYPE OF WAY—SODO AUSTIN

jail I forfeited the right to have interaction with the kids forfeited talking to them getting captured moments of them, seeing them, etc. Like with homies when there's no longer an interest involved, there's no longer an interest. (That interest being for her, your presence physically, sexually and financially (SMH)). I don't have a relationship with any of my 6 kids, it's technically 7, but one's suspect (maybe, maybe not). That's yet to be determined if he's actually mine, I can't say for certain, mama's baby, daddy's maybe! A DNA test, without a doubt, has to be taken to verify that, I'll never be foolish enough to just assume he's mine b'cuz of who his mother was/is and after catching her with her dude, potentially her son's biological. (Her late husband's homie who she's been in an off and on situationship with since his passing, which continued while she was with me, apparently and I'm sure it's still going on with them til this day under the guise of being her brother, like he was with me.) Oh, this is my brother such and such (SMH) bullshit ass bitch!

She was fucking this dude, but he was introduced to me as her brother (SMH). Not just by her, though, but by her sisters and a brother as well. (A real brother.) When she was pregnant with her baby (suspect), she was caught with this dude by me at a motel, there to fuck! That says a lot about her and who she is, if she's saying the baby she was carrying was mine. If in fact the baby was mine, why were you pregnant with my baby in your stomach fucking this dude? Either the baby wasn't mine and you were fucking the daddy, or it was mine and you were foul and raggedy! Either way, flag on the play! You can deny, which is what you're good at,

## FEELING SOME TYPE OF WAY—SODO AUSTIN

all you want that you weren't fucking ole boy until you're grey in the face, but you have to know who you're dealing with to think I would believe you weren't. You're not that good!

You could never convinced me otherwise or change my belief, not then, not today, not ever! At the end of the day, though, it's not even about you. It's really about knowing whether or not if you're last son is mine or isn't. At this point he's suspect, which is what I call him. One thing's for sure, he's definitely yours! But then I ask myself, should I even care, do it even matter? B'cuz I don't have a relationship with him nor do I know him, nor is there any type of feelings or emotions involved if I have to be perfectly honest with myself or the situation, as with the "3" I actually have with her. It's a complicated situation but it's something I had to disconnect from mentally and emotionally as a coping mechanism, as with disconnecting myself from so-called family, which came easy for me b'cuz I don't know them nor do they know me. There's no connection. We're literally strangers outside of sharing a bloodline which, as I'd stressed, means nothing and it wasn't by choice. I didn't pick the bloodline, I was born in it. I was told that the situation is partly on me b'cuz I chose not to reach out and should've. However, my argument is and will always be, people know where I am. I'm not hard to find or hard to pull up on.

How is it on me to reach out to them? I'm the one who's locked up and have been locked up for the past 20 years. They chose not to reach out and fuck with me and could've. Had ample opportunity on multiple occasions to pull up and get involved. So, with that being said, it is what it is. That line has been drawn in the sand already years ago and I'm cool with it, have been cool with it, "K.S.T.E.!" You want to know who else ain't shit? These police calling ass bitches, who call the police on niggahs without giving it a 2nd thought, for trivial shit. Especially in this climate we're in, in the world and in the United States especially, where the police are continuously killing unarmed black men and men of color. Quick to pick the phone up and dial 911! They don't realize the potential for that deadly confrontation. That's the last thing on their mind.

    They're not thinking of that possibility of a niggah being killed when the police pull up, b'cuz she's in her feelings and working with feelings, that thought never came into play. The last thing to enter her mind is the possibility of a niggah getting gunned down by a trigger happy ass white cop! Her whole thing, being in her feelings, is to get a niggah locked up on some get back (get even) type shit! (SMH) She's not thinking about the dynamics or ramifications of that phone call being potentially a death sentence instead of a jail sentence. It's bad enough they're putting dudes in Mickey situations over them. Dudes running up on dudes (approaching them) with static, wanting smoke (violence). Somebody's getting shot, stabbed or beat the fuck up! Or they're going to jail for killing a niggah! All behind this bitch being janky (scandalous), on her Mickey shit! (SMH)

    Where it really gets Mickey is when she gets a dude killed behind her shenanigans and she has to deal with those demons when she's alone in the dark and have to face them. Nobody else around, just her, and she has to be with herself and her thoughts, knowing she was the cause and the reason a niggah losing his life, and rightfully so, it's unshakable! You should be mentally tormented and have to struggle with that internally all while trying to keep up appearances, only you're not fooling anyone, though. You and I know what's going on. Knowing you're the one who put dude in harm's way...yeah, deal with it! (SMH) I don't care how much you drink, smoke weed, pop pills, or do gang drugs, you're never going to be able to numb that feeling or evade it. Its like when she's in her feelings and in her emotions, she has the worse case of the fuck its! Like a niggah do, will act on them without thought and she'll play ball as she see fit.

I'm a firm believer in the sentiment: "Ain't nothing like a bitch scorned!" She's playing ball! For sure. I've been a victim on the other side of that several times with baby mamas, all of whom called the police on me at one time or another (SMH). They'll call the police on you, set you up, lie on you, cross you, do physical harm to you, or have physical harm done to you. It doesn't matter if you're a husband, baby daddy, or just a niggah she in a situationship with. Dude she's actually laying down with at night and waking up to in the morning, yet claiming to love them, but in the same breath can contribute to their downfall or their demise (SMH). It gets real and gets Mickey. On some real shit, being in the streets and being who you are, you have to really be mindful of those you deal with and how you deal with them. Especially when you're being shown who they are by how they move and approach things b'cuz at that point you no longer have the argument or room to be in your feelings and emotions when that reality play out before you like a movie scene and it's bad.

## FEELING SOME TYPE OF WAY—SODO AUSTIN

I've seen these very movements and situations being approached, watching it in my situationship. Seeing how my "situation" (ex-wife) move, dealing with both her mother and brother being locked up, not once have I ever seen her write them, send them captured moments, send them energy (money or packages), accept any collect calls from them or go see them, let alone talk about either. With her, I got the look (her movement and how she approached the situation) firsthand. So, should I have expected anything different? You really know, if you've been through it with them b'cuz you already know what to expect... It's like you already know, but you're still expecting something different, which won't happen. Shame on you! It's not shame on them b'cuz you knew the deal. You knew they weren't fucking with you, while you were gone never pulled up on you. But as soon as they know you're out, they're fucking with you and have all the "convo" in the world for you...that's out! K.T.S.E.! We're all guilty of it, dealing with them when we know we shouldn't be dealing with them, based on their actions their attitude and knowing their demonstration while we were down. Somehow, though, we tend to fall back into that same ole trap, like it's been all gravity the whole time (SMH).

"Ayeee boy!"..."What up, mah niggah!"..."Sup, bay!" (SMH), bullshit ass people! (SMH) At the end of the day, you know you ain't shit! And you know what else? I ain't shit for fucking with you, knowing you ain't shit! Homie, if you're reading this and you know you're in the field of play, just be mindful and cautious of who you're interacting with and if you're cool with it...cool, but just know and overstand the likelihood of

## FEELING SOME TYPE OF WAY—SODO AUSTIN

you fucking with masks and images and when you fall, you know what it is. I guess on that note I'll park this pen, but never how I feel towards the contents and the realization of just how bullshit and disloyal people are that claim to love you, have love for you or fuck with you. (SMH)

    My whole perception and view of so-called family, homies and females I've interacted with are indicative of how they moved and expressed what and how they truly felt about T.I.C., teaching me a valuable lesson, as another one to grow on, which has drastically changed my attitude towards the whole so-called family, homies and relationship situation with females to a different degree and level of change. It's much deeper than just feelings and emotions and I'm not just going to call you "family" or "homie" or consider getting involved in a relationship with you just that easy. Those days are over. If the stars don't line up...we don't line up!

# Chapter 2

"A Snitch Anywhere Is A Threat To Real Niggahs Everywhere"

These are the fundamentals of a real street niggah's existence, .K.T.S.E. (Keep that same energy). You other dudes are irrelevant. It's unfortunate, though, that enthusiasm move the streets that so few enthusiastic can be trusted to speak on real shit or move real due to Autobotism and dirty pool that plague even the streets. You definitely have to be mindful of dudes, they're selling loyalty to the highest bidder. These are the dudes that snitches gravitate to b'cuz they know the loyalty is for sell. You have to be mindful of this dude anyway b'cuz your energy and verbals can be repeated. The next thing you know, the snitch has the upper hand and advantage to press play and it's Bluey-Bluey for you. Niggahs gon "sag you" (kill you or have you killed) based on you calling him a snitch and him knowing he's a snitch. You're the reminder, being verbal towards the situation, that matches the negative energy towards him, so his resort is to have you removed whether he does it or pay to have it done, he's intent on playing ball (harming you). That's his energy, get a bar.

I'm always saying it's levels to this shit! But at the end of the day, everything of value costs something to someone, in my mind. I'm still that same person in terms of how I'm wired. But yeah, you have to overstand it's not what you know, it's what you can prove and even then dudes will justify not pressing play (taking action) and will switch the game up. It's a dirty game for sure. Another nowadays you have to really reassess who

## FEELING SOME TYPE OF WAY—SODO AUSTIN

you can trust, especially when you have dudes fucking with snitches (SMH). I just don't get or overstand that look. It's really no excuse for dudes to fuck with a snitch, but that just shows you and expose the mentality and mindset. When you have to try and justify the reason you're fucking with s snitch, you know you're in a "no fly zone" and for that reason, I'm cool on you, b'cuz that's not a look I'm willing to have on my character. I'm going to distance myself completely from the equation, that's never a good look. "Oh, Tic's fucking with a niggah that fucks with a snitch!" That's no bueno! That'll never be the case, I'm 121% anti-snitch! Period, point blank! He's foreseen as a threat, him and those who fucking with him.

If that makes me a bad guy, so be it, I'll never wear that. Say hello to the bad guy! I know how to lose and I know how to win, so that's just what my movement is about. Overstanding can crystallize your vision and thought process when it comes to real things and real situations. On the flip side of that, you have a lot of bullshit dudes and Autobots included who're quick to put a snitch jacket on a niggah. Calling somebody a snitch is serious shit. The accusation is serious. It's not a word you use lightly b'cuz the consequences or ramifications are heavy. You can't just run around all "willy-nilly" (reckless abandon), accusing somebody of being a snitch and they aren't or you aren't sure. Suspected of being one and actually being one aren't one and the same. It's one thing to suspect it and another to voice it. All I'm saying is this, if you're voicing it, have the proof. It's like when you're on a yard and you accuse a dude of snitching, you have to produce the "work" (paperwork), for the most part.

You can't act on suspicion. Suspicion isn't going to cut it. It's so serious that if you can't produce the proof, the dude you're accusing of being a snitch is going to "pull up" (approach) on you in a real way. Which is what he's supposed to do, and if he doesn't it looks bad and gives dudes room to "politic him," have his name in their mouth and look at him as suspect. On some real shit, a niggah's "pressured up" to respond. No doubt, you don't have proof but you have a niggah's name in your mouth, a lot of time it's b'cuz of somebody else put it out there without proof and you're caught up on some Autobot shit (SMH). On top of that, who's to say there isn't a hidden agenda or dirty politics at play?

Moving along, let's venture into "dry snitching." Though it's indirect, it's borderline snitching. I mean, at the end of the day, it's saying shit you shouldn't be saying. Only difference is, you're not being direct with a name or individuals, but you're bringing awareness to a situation, having the police notice. It's so borderline that you could be "DP'ed" (disciplined) for it, given the right dudes that's around and looking at shit through a different lens, "Get a bar." From where I stand, we're in a maze that changes everything to the game, with a bad case of the fuck its! It's always a need to make adjustments, fucking with these dudes and their shenanigans though (SMH). Our actions and engagements have to be constantly adjusted.

So yeah, this horseplaying has been going on since Judas snitched on Jesus, the Sign of God, according to the Bible. Damn shame. (SMH)

## FEELING SOME TYPE OF WAY—SODO AUSTIN

Just like the title of this chapter says, "A Snitch Anywhere Is A Threat To Real Niggahs Everywhere." Not only is it a fact, but it's reality. Dudes manage, though, to "tell" for various reasons, even when they're not "pressured up" (police breathing heavy on them about a situation). Regardless of the reason, it'll never justify being a rat bastard. You're just a low down dirty vermin, a pretty fucked up individual to tell on the next dude. B'cuz you're weak and can't handle the consequences of playing the field, or being in the field of play. It's one thing I can say with a certainty, muthah fuckahs hate a snitch! "Oh, I can't go to jail. I didn't do it ass niggah!" (SMH) "I ain't going down for something I ain't do!" Yet you were with niggahs who did do something and y'all got caught up. You heard that saying, "If you fuckin' wit 'em, you duckin' wit 'em!" The right thing to do is ride it out and shut the fuck up! I don't need to repeat what the wrong thing is, but I will anyway. You don't snitch! So what you didn't do it, don't matter, your bad, it's the consequences of being in that life with niggahs who're about that life. I suggest you stay in your lane if your tolerance is low for being a stand up guy.

On the flip side of that, where a lot of dudes in the life go wrong, you know when dudes aren't built like that and playing "dress up," yet you'll have them around, seeing shit, hearing shit and knowing shit they shouldn't be privy to. I'm just calling a ball a ball and a strike a strike! But then act surprised when shit goes Mickey and go Bluey Bluey (bad), they're telling. When a niggah tells you, "Oh, I'm not with that," or "That's not what I'm about!" take the dude at his word, he's telling you then, "If something happens or if I'm pressured up, I'm telling." You just weren't trying to hear him, so caught up on whatever you were on. He told you, though: "I'm telling, I'm not going to jail!" Yeah, wrap your mind around that the next time you're pressuring a niggah to do something, you know and he knows he's not with, it's a crash waiting to happen.

For certain, everyone isn't built for that pressure of being pressed in that interrogation room by detectives breathing heavy on them. They'll even think of some other shit to tell, that has nothing to do with why they're there in the first place. "I know about a situation and who's involved!" ...Whaaat! It's so many dudes that have been caught up in that same situation, then it's: "I know about this murder... I know where someone is that's on the run!" (SMH) Some shit he had nothing to do with, but knows the details and who the players are or were (SMH). Damn dummies! Next thing niggahs know, detectives are pulling up (SMH). If the spotlight weigh a ton, pressure weigh even more. Different variations but basically all the same melody. Here's an instance, if you're having a "set" (gang) meeting and homies that are active and with the "festivities" (putting in work on the enemigos) are discussing strategy on how to move and who's going to be doing what, when and where. You don't have homies that aren't with that, sitting in the meeting, getting a bar (listening). What would his purpose be being there getting a bar? He's playing no role in anything. He's not participating in the festivities. Personally, I don't see the logic, nor does it make any sense to me for him being there. What are the odds of that having a fucked up outcome down the road? Dudes fall out of favor all of the time just like situations popping up and dudes aren't

## FEELING SOME TYPE OF WAY—SODO AUSTIN

trying to go to jail, get a bar (pay attention). To you, oh, he's the homie, he's straight. To me it's a bad idea waiting to turn into a situation.

How many homies you know that have gotten caught up just b'cuz of a dude knowing something he had no part in, but found himself in a Mickey (tricky) situation and instead of taking his situation like a champ, he speaks on something he knew about? Shit...I know personally, the shit happened to me by a niggah blood related. The niggah straight "horseplayed" (told). Yeah, I know... Whaaat! Flag on the play! I felt the same way. Never in my wildest dream would I ever have thought this niggah was a snitch, would ever snitch, would've thought to snitch, yet here I sit in prison with a life sentence. It was like he went out of his way to snitch on me (SMH). My shit had nothing to do with what he had going on whatsoever, but here it is: "I know where somebody is that the Long Beach police are looking for!" We're in a whole different city, miles away from Long Beach. Cold niggah, though! (SMH) What I can't get out of my mind, though, is the fact he told over some misdemeanor type shit.

Some shit that carried no serious time, if any (SMH). Switching lanes, though, I don't respect or condone suicide in general, for any reason. Killing yourself just ain't it! Especially a dude taking his own life b'cuz he's not trying to go to jail, or even while in jail and can't handle his time. I'm like this, at the end of the day, though, handle your "wax" (consequences) when shit go south and I don't mean to Georgia. That's just what a real niggah do. He doesn't cave or fold to pressure like a lawn chair with a fat bitch trying to sit on it, b'cuz shit got Mickey. He take his shit on the chin and keep pushing (moving).

## FEELING SOME TYPE OF WAY—SODO AUSTIN

I've been in a few situations and kept it solid. It wasn't a question. That's just how I'm built, I'm not built for snitching, it's just not in me, never have been, never will be, under no circumstances. On this other note, though, why be something or somebody you're not and sabotaging the universal plot if you're not about that life? Me personally, if I put myself in a Mickey situation and it goes Bluey Bluey (bad/sideways) I'm going to take what I have coming. It's as simple as that. Snitching isn't an option nor is suicide, whether self-inflicted or by a cop, that's out! I can accept the consequences for what and as they are. I played the game of chance and it cost me, period. I knew what I was signing up for. My mentality is this: "I fucked up, I got caught, it is what it is." The easy way out is a bitch niggah way out! I pride myself in being loyal, solid, and a stand up type of guy. Anything less than that is a mis-overstanding and goes against the code of ethics.

Snitching in my opinion is viewed as a weak emotion and rightfully so, just based on being in a situation and your go to is the emotional state of weakness. Which also, in my opinion, was always dormant inside of you. It was just waiting to present itself. These are truths that are hard to face and are ugly and at odds with how "we" (street niggahs) feel shit should be, according to our code of conduct, being who we are, being out there in the field. Situations as they manifest will no doubt give you that sense of realization. Like trying to get your head around the fact, dudes harbor snitches and condone their pernicious behavior as if it's cool. There is nothing cool or fly about condoning snitching or harboring a snitch. That's no bueno and a no fly zone! Fuck

## FEELING SOME TYPE OF WAY—SODO AUSTIN

having the ability to see it or overstand it from the other side. Ain't that much ability or overstanding in the world, that's out! That's a niggah who's heart ain't right. I'm a firm believer in the sentiment: "If a niggah's heart ain't right, ain't no telling what the fuck he'll do!" ...Dudes get in situations and then want to shift the weight (SMH).

It's just crazy to me, though, how dudes will know a niggah's snitching and still let him be in the "set" (neighborhood or the yard). (SMH) This dude's a rat bastard and it's in black-and-white (documented on paperwork, transcript or otherwise). Not only is it documented but the shit is viral and went viral (everybody knows), the set knows, so it's in the streets, thus in the county jail to the prison yards, it's no secret. Dudes act like they don't know the nature of the game they're in. I can think of a few more instances where shit seem more like an exclamation point than a question mark. The thing that gets me the most is dudes can know a dude's a snitch and have the audacity to have the attitude that he didn't tell on me, so fuck it! ...Whaaat! If you don't knock it off, pick it back up and knock it off again! You sound stupid as fuck! Where is the logic in that mindset? The shit's so crazy, though, nowadays snitches can basically "feed" the right niggah's and be allowed to have a presence in the set or on the yard. It's all gravity (good), dudes are willing to look the other way, basically turn a blind eye, for some energy (financial gain or incentives). It didn't use to be that way (SMH), niggahs were voted off the island! Some tend to believe, it's the gang drugs contributing to the decline of the stand up, solid and loyal guy.

## FEELING SOME TYPE OF WAY—SODO AUSTIN

Then you have cases where bias plays a role in dudes overlooking the fact that a dude is a rat. "That's my bro!" "That's my unc!" "That's my this or that!" Yeah, that might be, but it doesn't change the facts of who he is or the dynamics of the situation. He's still going to be your "bro," your "unc," or however he's connected to you, he's a rat! ...Still! Not only are you being biased but you're still fucking with this dude like he's straight (cool), and still hanging out in traffic with him, with the mindset: "I just have to navigate my movements and activities around him," or "I'll only fuck with him to an extent." That's out! I'm not fucking with him to no extent, I don't do rats! Cousin, Brother, Uncle, that's a no fly zone with me! Let him get "fly" (tell) on you, though, then it's an issue, now he's a rat and scum of the Earth. (SMH) Sammy the Bull and any other name associated with snitching, it shouldve been an issue "off the dribble" (from get go/the beginning).

You know what's even crazier? You could hang with a muthah fuckah everyday and still not know what he might do. When the sun go down, he's a shadow niggah of a different kind. You don't repay loyalty with betrayal. Truth is, though, at the end of the day I no longer put nothing past anybody. What can you really do when shit happens by forces already in motion? Stick to the script and to the code. Sow an act and you reap a habit. Sow a habit and you reap a character. Sow a character and you reap loyalty, morals and standards. Don't let anything or anyone isolate you from the reality of what it is to be solid, loyal and a stand up guy.

## FEELING SOME TYPE OF WAY—SODO AUSTIN

Due to a space that's constantly changing, motivated by gang drugs coupled with all of the other "dysfunctions" (shenanigans, Autobotism, dirty politics, etc.). Having the right gears are essential to being able to navigate your way. It's a whole different culture, you either find your way or lose your way! I personally won't compromise where things matter to me, add up or count. Character is everything. Bottom line, you're with the snitch shit, you can hit the exit! You should've felt that coming b'cuz it was premeditated. The same way you premeditated your telling, making your conscious decision to get a niggah wrapped up with them "boys" (police) (SMH), that's just what and how I feel about the situation. Standing in truth means calling dudes on shit they rather keep under wraps. It is what it is, though. Dudes need to be called on their "Gilliganism" (another term for bullshit and fuckery).

It's been a discrepancy with police reports over the years. As far as the validity of them and whether or not they count, b'cuz the police could be suspect at times with putting whatever in them to pit whatever narrative they need according to some. True but debatable, it does leave room for argument, however it can also be an attempt to justify a situation. However, my position is this: on some street niggah shit, if you make any type of statement, that's considered "talking" (telling). There's no refuting that, thus making the "report" valid of what it is, period. You made a statement which they advise you, "You have the right not to," especially without a lawyer being present. When it's all said and done, you're not supposed to make no statement! Whatsoever.

## FEELING SOME TYPE OF WAY—SODO AUSTIN

It's never a good look, nor a good thing, to have nothing in black-n-white with your name on it, it's a bad look. Period, point blank. You're putting a label on yourself, making yourself a target of politics, giving politicians ammo to politic you. When you make that bed, you have to lay in that bed. It's the cost of going against the grain, being in direct violation. So to answer the question: Do they count? Shit, "paperwork" is "paperwork" at the end of the day, is it not? You made a statement, it's on paper, it's no getting around that. That's what it is. I don't see how it's not counted as paperwork. I don't see how it's even an issue to debate. I've had arguments over this very subject, but if you don't knock it off, though, it's telling! Yeah, we know how police will or can put a twist on words, especially if you don't play ball or won't play ball, which is a tactic. But the reality is it derived from a statement. They can't add shit if there wasn't nothing to add to. I was privy to more than a few police reports and was asked my opinion on the contents under the guidelines of telling. First and foremost, it was too much content to read. A single line is too much, but what I viewed, yeah, definitely. "What happened was!" (SMH) If you don't make a statement, there's nothing for you to try to explain later or defend. "What I meant was such and such, my words were twisted!" (SMH)

How about you exercise your rights to shut the fuck up! Just saying...you're unquestionably in violation. "Hear no evil, see no evil, speak no evil!" Know this, you'll only avoid the inevitable conclusion for so long. The timer's been set, with you're telling ass! For those who're condoning the conduct, being complicit in it or on some "look the other way type shit," you're just as foul and bullshit, with a major character flaw, as the rat niggah! What about citizens? What about them? Though snitching ain't cool, period, citizens aren't held and can't be held to the same standard or code. They aren't in the life. Who's tripping on Mrs. Johnson's nosy ass peeking out her blinds as she always does and calling the police, b'cuz homies are "thick" (a lot of individuals) hanging out, drinking and smoking weed, maybe a couple are "slanging" (selling) weed or dope?

    If you're hanging out though, and functioning with dude, you're suuuper foul and you're bullshit (SMH). I'll conclude this chapter with this. All the rules are "null and void" except on: snitching! As I'd stressed in "Yard Life," it's just a no fly zone! Period! So you know, you're energy is the fuel for this real shit and for those that have a problem with my being vocal, as I am on this explosive subject, I stand on what I stand on. "Hate it or love it," "Right or wrong," "Thick or thin," it's always everyday all day! ...Recognotice! (Recognize and notice) "Dry or wet" (dry snitching -- indirect, wet snitching -- direct) It's snitching and I'm gon call a ball a ball and a strike a strike...

# Chapter 3

## "Yard Life"

Yeah, the homie Young Ace Capone, yellow retarded ass from the set ("Young Found Crip"/"Insane Crip"), finally resurrected from the "sandbox" after doing a nine month SHU term for assaulting the police, which stemmed from the situation with Get Drunk (a use-to-be homie from 20's) tapping out (going S.N.Y.). We were (the homies) trying to figure out what would make him tap out. We couldn't figure it out. He was solid all the way around the board, outside of getting drunk and not being able to hold his liquor. What ended up being speculated though, was that he felt as though he had an issue coming behind Young Ace Capone's situation with the police and him basically not getting involved. But who's to say for certain? I don't know what's going on on the "lower yard" with the homies in 2 Building. On another note though, word was he (Get Drunk) used me, the homie Ace, the homie H.2.O. from 20's and the lil homie Lil Young Ken Dog from the set (Baby's/Insane Crip) as escape goats to go S.N.Y., saying we (the homies) were going to gang rape him and stab him up...what the fuck! Yeah, he was horseplaying for real with that!

If that wasn't some crazy shit! When I heard the shit, I was surprised the "goon squad" hadn't pulled up on us for being implemented in that scenario (SMH). I didn't overstand, of all the things that could've been said, why was that said? However, it didn't go viral. It stayed amongst the homies (SMH). I got the "play" (situation) from the homie

## FEELING SOME TYPE OF WAY—SODO AUSTIN

Dirty Mike from the 20's when I called to tap in with him on the streets, who got it directly from H.2.O. when he (H.2.O) tapped in (called) with him. When all of this went on, we hadn't had program, so I wasn't able to get the scoop on what happened with the homies at that time. So I had to wait to get it direct. Then finally H.2.O. was able to pull up on the "upper yard" from the lower yard to fill me in, which he'd done. He told me himself what Get Drunk had said. (SMH)

  Yeah, that fucked me up. "Ain't no plans with a man, homie!" I'm into bitches! We (me and Cal) were sitting in the cell and the homie Vamp 3 from 92 Hoover (Nine-Deuce) pulled up on the cell door, telling us Ace was getting out of the sandbox and was single cell status, but needed a "spot" (cell) to go to. There was no one trying to move to the lower yard, so him moving in our building was a no go. No bueno. The police ended up moving the homie back to his old building (2 Building) on the lower yard. A day later when we came out the building for yard, one of the Hoover homies, Lon or Vamp, let us know that Ace was on the "patio." Cal made his way to the patio to holler at him. Me and HL (Hoover Lon) had already made it to the "slab" (concrete slab) and were "bussing down" (working out), when Cal and Ace came through the yard door twenty minutes later. The police wouldn't let Ace all the way on the yard but allowed him to walk with Cal a few feet from the yard door, underneath the tower, which is where me and HL met them. We chopped it up (talked) for a few minutes before the police was on him, telling him he had to get back to his side of the yard. We dapped and he left, throwing up treys

## FEELING SOME TYPE OF WAY—SODO AUSTIN

(three fingers). I really didn't get to holler at him like I wanted to but told him we'll holler and we'll be working on getting him moved on our side of the yard. We tried getting Pac to move on the upper yard after H.2.O. left, but he was cool staying on the lower yard.

But yeah, I needed to see where Ace's mind was on a couple of things, which we got cleared up later. I like to address issues instead of letting them linger. Basically, I was confused about why the pulled up to my door asking me if I was cool if Peacock could move in the cell with me. Without a doubt I told them, "Why wouldn't it be cool? He's my homie. Just send him!" So, they put his name tag with his picture on it on the wall next to the cell door and walked away, happy that I accepted him. That's the thing with me though. I accept homies whether they're from my "tribe" (set) or a Crip homie. I don't turn away Crips though, period. You can come in if you choose to stay cool, if your homies "pull you" (move you where they are), cool too. It'll get figured out. A lot of dudes off the dribble won't accept you and basically have the police find you somewhere to go. To me, that's bullshit and you're a bullshit ass niggah! The Crip factor aside, dude is Black. (SMH)

So yeah, the police are accustomed to these bullshit ass niggahs' shenanigans. We're the only race that plays these types of games. The other races off top, it's a "no fly zone" (no turning away anyone that comes to your door. Whatever needs to get figured out, it will.) All that, a dude coming to the door and being told: "Hell naw!" That's no bueno! Yet, dudes wonder why the police act certain ways and move certain ways when it comes to us (Blacks). B'cuz of bullshit niggahs and their

## FEELING SOME TYPE OF WAY—SODO AUSTIN

shenanigans! They see there's no unity or structure, none at all! Tell the truth, shame on the devil. So yeah, the other issue was with the homie (Ace) while he was in the sandbox he had heard the homie Crip-Cal had landed on the yard. I'm assuming from the homie Dirty Mike, due to him staying logged in (communicating on a regular) with him through the mail, sending him (Crip-Cal) his love and respects. But not through Mike, through another Crip homie that left the sandbox a week or so prior to coming out himself. I took issue with it, for the simple fact he knew not only I was still on the yard, but me and Cal now were cellies. I felt he was being funny or had an issue with me. So me being in my head already, with him not coming to the cell, then not hollering at me but hollered at the homie. Yeah, definitely felt he was on some Gilligan shit and was going to address it. We talked though, and it was all gravity (good). He ended up moving to our building and in our section (B-Section) on the lower tier in cell 120, solo b'cuz of his single cell status. A couple of days later, Cal went to medical and when he came back he was telling me a few "I.E." (Inland Empire) cats he knew from Wasco Reception Center he came up here with pulled up (approached him) on him with some shit about the homie Pac (Pac-10) from 20's (Long Beach 20's).

    He heard them out, seeing what they had to say, as he should've. They're doing their due diligence, following protocol (addressing an issue before taking it into their own hands). At the end of the day though, the homie's innocent until proven guilty. He has that coming. Unless the dynamic is him admitting to what's being alleged, in which case the homie did. He admitted to doing "bunk" (doing something that he shouldn't have) (SMH). His exact words being, "I did bunk! The I.E. cats said that Pac had the police go in their homie's cell after he went to the sandbox under a guise and got his TV. (The guise was Pac saying the TV was his and for the police to allow him to get it, for them not to pack it.) Taking Pac's word, the police allowed him to go in dude's cell and get the TV. (SMH) Clearly, a violation on the homie's part. What he was thinking, who knows? But that was no bueno!

So the situation was discussed amongst the homies, which only consisted of myself, Young Ace Capone and Cal, 3 Insanes. H.2.O left for court and has been gone a month or so, up to this point. So, Cal and Ace went to the lower yard to look into the situation with the homie. I say, though, after leaving the upper yard, it couldn't have been more than a good ten minutes when the alarm went off and the yard tower police was yelling, "Geeettt dooowwwn!" on the lower yard, then on the upper yard, and as police were running from the buildings, we could hear the police on the lower yard yelling for someone to get down! Then bloooom! More yelling. Bloooom! "Geeettt dooowwwn!" Bloooom! Don't know for sure if it was the homies at first, suspected it though, even though it was as quick as it was. It didn't appear to have been long enough to have looked into the situation, but then, it goes back to Pack admitting he done something he shouldn't have and he was "got on" (DP'ed). The kicker though, and what fucked the homies up (surprised them), Pac had a banger (a knife) on him, which ended up on the ground next to Pac. Oh, this niggah was gon play ball! (SMH) The goon squad pulled up as only they do when a weapon is involved. Neither Ace nor Cal was stuck (stabbed) though. But just based on it was an incident and a weapon was found, they were pulling up. When I heard the goon squad was involved, from a Bay Area dude that pulled up on me letting me know it was the homies, it surprised me b'cuz they were only going to the lower yard to holler at the homie, to see what the deal was and get to the bottom of the fiasco.

Afterwards, when they left the yard and were in the cages inside of the "substation" (program office), Cal and Ace were like Pac was in his F and E's (feelings and emotions) about the situation and "popping it" (talking about shit and making threats) (SMH). Ace and Cal came back to the yard and Pac went to the sandbox for the banger (SMH). The general consensus was watch Pac, try and put it out there like it was on some gang banging shit! Which it clearly wasn't, but that's dudes' go to when they're in the wrong or in their feelings and then the Autobotism comes into play. Now it's a whole different narrative. Niggahs is gang banging! (SMH) How about, "A niggah stole and he got DP'ed!" and, "Keeping it 1000, he got off light b'cuz it was technically a ball playing offense." I saw dudes get ball played on them for stealing. That's calling a ball a ball and a strike a strike. Gang banging had nothing to do with the situation...period!

A few days after that occurred, me, Lon and the homie Ace were on the slab bussing down. Three Damus (Bloods) were on the slab bussing down next to us. After being on the slab for almost an hour, they (3 Damus) pushed (left). As they were walking, two of the Damus squared off and then started squabbling up (fighting) in the field. One of the Damus that wasn't involved was waved off, like: "Stand down, my niggah,

## FEELING SOME TYPE OF WAY—SODO AUSTIN

it's me and your homie, it has nothing to do with you!" Initially though, he acted like he wanted to get involved b'cuz, at the end of the day, it was his homie squabbling (fighting) from the set. The yard got put down. "Geeettt dooowwwn!" The police ran from the buildings towards them. As they're running towards them they're yelling for them to get down, but to no avail, then bloooom!

    A smoke grenade gets thrown at them, they're still going. Bloooom! A second one goes off. After the second one goes off, one of them gets down and is quickly searched and cuffed, being sat on his "back pockets" (butt). The other one refused and started walking towards the "Black area," towards the tables. As he's walking, the police are following him and yelling for him to get down, which he ignores and keeps moving towards the tables. "Blood, this is some bullshit!" He's leading the police towards the Blacks, not being considerate and mindful of what anybody else has going on. As he gets closer to the tables he removes his situation and drops it on the dirt and kicks it. The police see the play (movement) and once he gets down, they search and cuff him, then had a search grid going on in the Black area, searching every Black in and around the area and searching property that was around (clothing items, bags, etc.).

    The outcome "2" Blacks were caught, having weapons on them (SMH). They were led off of the yard to the substation on their way to the sandbox. An older Damu, T-Ro up out of San Diego, a real gentleman and a scholar, apologized to all of the Blacks in our area for the Gilliganism on his homies part and Gilliganism it was (SMH). You walked away from the

## FEELING SOME TYPE OF WAY—SODO AUSTIN

incident with the police following you to the Black area, drop and kick something. What were you thinking? What did you think was gon happen? Everybody on the yard saw that outcome coming a mile away. Without a doubt, the police was going to search the area, along with every Black person in or near the vicinity. No mystery there (SMH). Dudes were clowning about that situation for days, even the Ese's (Southern Hispanic).

Damn homies, I thought that vato was walking the track! (SMH) Yeah, I'll never overstand where his brain was or what cylinder he was functioning on. "You got it, it's yours!" You don't pull nobody into your Mickey situation. Flag on the play! That comes with riding like that (riding dirty). If you're about that life, be about the consequences of that life. These antics and shenanigans around High Desert never cease to amaze me (SMH). That situation for certain went viral (being talked about and will be talked about for a while). ...Whaaat! Yeah, that was "DTM" (doing too much)...all day long! It'll get figured out. Everybody's question though, was...why? And what was that about? I'm surprised he didn't get shot b'cuz, for all they knew, you could've been trying to attack someone. You're moving towards a group of people who're down on the ground and, mind you, they were told to "prone out" on their stomach, so they're really vulnerable (SMH). It's a lot of variables that played into him, possibly becoming a victim, it really surprised me the police didn't "buss" (shoot). But then again, not really... I've never seen that before (SMH). Again, just when you think you've seen it all, here comes something else to prove to you, you hadn't. Gilliganism and shenanigans are continuous and real. You'll be in a constant state of whoa! Unbelievable! That's where I was

## FEELING SOME TYPE OF WAY—SODO AUSTIN

with it as I watched the scene play out before me on the yard. (SMH) Real comedy, how I knew those individuals though, didn't find nothing funny about the situation...not at all! They were sitting in the sandbox along with him, which was preventable (SMH). One thing's for certain, two things for sure, they'll be more mindful of how they do what they do! You can't leave your security (securing your security) in the next dude's hands. Shit's too unpredictable, especially with how the next dude moves on the yard...clearly! And It'll be the fluke (unintentional) that gets you caught up...real shit!

(SMH) This shit is just crazy, how you have to keep an eye and side eye on certain dudes when they're characters and aren't moving right, which you'll notice, he's noticeable b'cuz it's a lot of Gilliganism going on with him. You can tell when a dude need someone to basically baby sit him, b'cuz he can't be trusted to move accordingly without supervision. You literally have these types running around on the yard (SMH). This dude's a liability b'cuz you never know what he might do and when he might do it. When he feels he's not being watched he's unpredictable, when no one's around or when no one's watching him. He'll get it in his mind, it's whatever! It's not whatever though homie, b'cuz it's bigger than you. It's not about just you. What you do is a reflection on the whole (homies).

Which can have the whole caught up in some shit, all b'cuz you decided to be a Gilligan. It's cool though, if that's what you choose to do, but accept what you got coming. When you got it coming, ain't no calling flag on the play! You had that coming. Me and the homie had a

## FEELING SOME TYPE OF WAY—SODO AUSTIN

conversation the other day about how niggahs have the audacity and nerve to be in their feelings and emotions when they get "DP'ed" for something. Niggah, you're the one in violation. Ain't that a bitch! Then they want to rally the Autobots and spin the narrative...bullshit niggah! It's been a few homies pull up since H.2.O left for court. Menace from North Side Long Beach, Sex.Money.Murder, a civilian named Chance off the East Side and an older homie named Mel from 20's. Menace and Chance are on the lower yard. Haven't had the chance to holler at either of them but plan to face to face. However, I sent a "one-time" (note) to Menace introducing myself to him and Chance, letting them know what homies are on the upper yard and seeing if they were trying to come on the upper yard, or if they were cool being on the lower. They both indicated they were straight being where they were. Say no more (no need to further discuss it). As with everyone who lands on the yard, the "work" (paperwork) is looked at and the script on how we're functioning is relayed. "Don't do debts, if you do anything be sure you can cover it. We don't fuck with the police (cursing out or disrespecting the police or arguing with them) and we don't involve ourselves in shit that jeopardizes the 'car' (homies) or doesn't concern Long Beach! Outside that, it's just yard life. Dudes doing and being them, moving through the 'maze'. When it comes to an issue or issues with the homies, the collective have an input on it, it's a democracy not a dictatorship. We're not doing the 'key' thing (one person having say-so on what happens with a situation with a homie. We all have to be in agreement). However, different yards move different. This is just how we're moving on D-yard in High Desert, and with that, majority rules."

## FEELING SOME TYPE OF WAY—SODO AUSTIN

If the majority say "No" on a play it's "No" on a play! Period, fall back (leave it alone/it's not happening). If the majority say you're voted off the island, you're voted off the island. Thee majority rules every time. The majority is recognoticed as law...period. Those who were overruled, it's nothing personal, it never is. It's just business, regardless of feelings, personal or otherwise. But one thing's for sure, if it's a situation that comes about involving a homie from the City. Another tribe, or member from another tribe can't dictate or have us "pressured up" as to how we DP our homie(s) or how we conduct Long Beach business. You're from where you're from and we're from where we're from. Long Beach! If you present a situation, we'll address it accordingly. Anything outside of that is a misoverstanding.

You have no input, influence or voice in what Long Beach got going on. The strangest shit I've seen in my 20 years of being on yards was a Northern Crip from Stockton accepting a DP even though it was nothing but "laps" from another Crip out of L.A. (SMH). ...Whaaat! That was really strange and weird to me, something I wouldn't have ever went for in a gazillion years. That's out! ...Whaaat! Wish a niggah would! You're not from my tribe, you're not my homie a you're not from my city. You're just another dude or dudes pushing C.R.I.P.! That was no bueno, flag on the play! But that's the type of stunts you'll have an it's only you and 2 other homies from your tribe on the yard, if you allow it. You can blame it on dude being young and naive, but that shouldn't have played out like that regardless of what the situation was, period! The craziest shit though,

## FEELING SOME TYPE OF WAY—SODO AUSTIN

young homie had to "run laps" b'cuz he lied about something he wasn't with (having a banger) when he was asked about having one.

The thing is, homie that asked won't have one or use one, from my overstanding, but will squabble all day. This much I know to be true, he'll no doubt squabble with you (fight). First off though, why are you "banger checking me"? You're not my homie, you're not from my tribe and you're not from my city. More importantly, why is it any of your business whether or not I have one? That shouldn't concern you homie! With all due respect, that's the whole thing. Dudes shouldn't know if you have one or not. You never know, this may be a dude you get into it with, but now the gig is up. He knows you're strapped (armed), so he knows how to approach the confrontation prior to. (SMH) But yeah, I just felt I should share that scenario b'cuz it was one for the books! Switching lanes (get a bar), of a WTF (what the fuck) moment...what the fuck is going on in the minds of a lot of these dudes around here on the yard? Why do these same mentally challenged dudes think that they are so damn slick that somebody would believe the bullshit and Gilliganism that comes out of their mouths over what was witnessed by somebody's eyes?

For real, what the fuck is in the water being drunk that has some of these so-called rational dudes thinking on the same level as the chemically dependent ones??? I mean, for the love of Allah, I thought this was a men's prison, but more and more I'm seeing guys in single cells sitting on their toilets "reverse cowgirl" style to pee, and I can't help but think to myself, "What the fuck is all that about?" Now here's a real damn it all! What's the deal with one of the worse accusations under the sun being leveled at a man and he just denies its validity, yet doesn't appear to be the least bit upset at being questioned about his moral compass being beneath the scale of depravity???

Now if one was judging based on reaction, how could you think anything other than, "What the fuck?"!!! Being an observant man, I watch and study dudes' character, so when I see other dudes come up and shake hands with known Gilligans, I just shake my head and laugh as I think to myself, "What the fuck?" Birds of a feather really do flock together. It's what bullshit dudes and Autobots do, they flock together on one accord, bird ass niggahs! They're feather to feather, one can't and don't fully exist or function without the other, which is what I've come to over stand visually as well (SMH). It really saddens me b'cuz these dudes are lost causes...truly! The other night we had an older Crip from Raymond Ave Crip who pulled up from off the bus from somewhere. They (the police) tried to put him in the cell with the young Stockton Crip who'd been turning down Crips since he moved back in our section (B Section) after moving back from off the lower yard.

First he came with the (excuse) he's not accepting no lifers, then went to he don't want a cellie period. But from my observation, every Crip that has come to his door was a Down South Crip (L.A., Long Beach, etc.) and he refused them. He refused 2 of my homies for sure. We even told him it would only be for a short time, just until we found them a spot in the building. He had an issue with it, so it never happened. The first time was like hesitation, which was observed, so the homie was like, "Fuck it," and moved on. He felt the homie was tripping and felt the need to explain.

## FEELING SOME TYPE OF WAY—SODO AUSTIN

They talked and he told the homie, "If another one of your homies come or a Crip, it was good." Ace was getting out of the sandbox and needed a spot. Weird Cuz was approached and he was with the shenanigans again. It worked out b'cuz what we didn't know, Ace couldn't move with him anyway. He was single cell status (couldn't have a cellie), but it just exposed Weird Cuz was still on his weird shit! (SMH)

So, naturally, my mind immediately goes to he's not celling up with no Down South Crip, being an Up North Crip. I've ran into a few cool ones, but the majority of them I've encountered were weird. Him not wanting lifers as a cellie was bullshit! The older Crip had a lower-lower chrono (you have to be on the lower tier and on the bottom bunk due to a medical issue). So this is what Weird Cuz do, he refused to let him in the cell and while the police only stood 15 feet or so away, he started getting loud and animated with the older Crip, drawing attention, and once the police asked what was the problem, Weird Cuz was like, "He can't come in here, I'm not taking him." (SMH) That wasn't a good look. Fuck the fact he was Crip, he was Black, period! You had other races commenting on it like, "That's not cool, fool!" He straight caused a scene but like with everything else around here, it'll get addressed for certain as soon as the yard is open. No doubt, he'll be pulled up on. Yard's been janky lately b'cuz of us being on a rolling lockdown (one day on, one day off) and due to staff shortages, so the yard been hit and miss.

When it was all said and done though, they couldn't find the older Crip a cell, so H.L. (Hoover Lon) got at one of his younger Hoover homies (8-Ball from Five-Nine) to take him, at least until he can make

## FEELING SOME TYPE OF WAY—SODO AUSTIN

other arrangements. But yeah, since the incident, ole boy (Weird Cuz) has been getting the cold shoulder from most of the Blacks in our section and is feeling some type of way b'cuz he recognotice. He really need to do it moving back to the lower yard where the NC's (Northern Crips) are or move with his only homie in C-Section. His other homie he had in C-Section just left and went to C-Yard under suspicious circumstances, as far as what's being spoke on. Knowing something had to get said to the police, convincing enough to get you moved off of the yard. B'cuz you don't just moved like that from off of this yard especially. With a simple request? ...That's no bueno! Something was said to get moved.

    The only way you leave this yard is you land in the Intake Building (8 Building) and the police move you to C-Yard b'cuz there's space over there for you. Or you leave a victim (whupped up off the yard). All I know is he went to the "patio" to the pm (night) pill call and lagged back and never returned to the building. WTF! (SMH). I'm guessing he got into his own head like a lot of dudes do and became paranoid over thinking what he had going on and his mind started playing tricks on him. He did owe some rabbs (money) and then come to find out he was pushing Crip when actually he wasn't one. No one questioned it, but then when it came to light he wasn't, he was told to stop saying Cuz! He was caught saying it again after the fact and was pulled up on about it. I'm thinking he spooked himself (SMH).

    As I stressed, a lot of dudes get in their own heads until their mind begins playing tricks on them, feeling as though they're being plotted on. Especially when they know they've done something the shouldn't have or

## FEELING SOME TYPE OF WAY—SODO AUSTIN

just playing with the game (doing shit for no rhyme or reason) inside the maze. If you really think about it, this prison shit, this yard shit is mostly mental (mind over matter) and with that you have to have a strong mind to maintain. The physical aspect of it is easy to do. Shit...we grew up fighting and getting jumped. I never overstood and still don't, how when a dude decides to tap out behind a DP (physical DP), whether he had one coming or already been DP'ed. (SMH) At the end of the day, it's over with once it happens or it happened. Its just you're being told, "Aye, slow your roll! DMT (doing too much). You're fucking up, get your shit together before you find yourself voted off the island!"

Accept it and keep it moving! Don't turn a situation into a worse situation b'cuz you're in your head and it results in an action you can't come back from. B'cuz once you go S.N.Y, your career (life in prison or on the yard as you knew it) is O.V.E.R.! That part! (SMH) Which brings me to this point with a conversation I just had recently with my Bay Buddy Hersh the other day about how dudes go S.N.Y. that's been thugging on the line (mainline) for years, were solid and reputable homies. How dudes still communicate and fuck with them like they're still active and cool after taking that walk of shame. Still considering these dudes homies! (SMH) "He's still the homie!" ...Whaaat? He's still the homie? This dude left the line with real niggahs, the last of them to be on the line with a bunch of weirdos and dropouts. How does that even equate? Really though!

Hersh was like the crazy part is, when these dudes get out and go back to the streets, they're still going to be accepted in the set by homies, horseplaying as if him being in prison on an S.N.Y. yard didn't exist (SMH). His (Hersh) whole attitude was like dudes need to knock that shit off! Dudes shouldn't be messing with them (dudes that went S.N.Y.), let alone acknowledging them as homies that count and looking out for them, sending them energy! That should be no bueno! It's more in agreement than not with the sentiment. That shit's just not cool. He forfeited his receiving any type of homie love and energy the day he decided to take that walk. Me personally, I don't overstand dudes' mind states when it comes to morality, the way they can just allow bias to carry and have weight over what's right, b'cuz of their personal relationship or connection to a dude (SMH), blatantly dismissing the fact that he went S.N.Y. The same dude that's politicking and tripping when it's the next dude! It's "He has walked the plank!" "It's over for him!" "He fucked up!" "He bet (better) not ever come back to the set." (SMH) The same dude that's talking bad about dudes who went S.N.Y. or are S.N.Y.! Like a dude politicking another dude for snitching but is harboring a snitch and trying to stop an issue he has coming to him (SMH). That's out! ...Suuuper! Me and the homie were in the cell talking about our BM's this morning as we do. We were on how they have a similar situation going on or went on as far as them (BM's) having kids in the system or having been in the system and them not fighting to get them back when they were taken, basically giving up, or not trying hard enough to get them back.

Being content with not having them (the kids) b'cuz of having that freedom to live life and to suck, fuck, smoke and drink without having that responsibility. Being caught up in their life in their world, enjoying their happiness and being happy to where the kids became non-factors and nonexistent (SMH). He was telling me how his (BM) has multiple kids in the system and she's so unfit and bullshit, if she were to get pregnant and child services were to hear about it they're pulling up. "Let me get that!" (Give me the baby) We also were talking about how daddies are being called and considered sperm donors for not being in their kids' lives. But what about the "birther" (a girl who carries a child for 9 months but has no maternal or undying connection to them)? You're no better than a sperm donor. You carried the child and can just walk away from them without looking back over your shoulder, won't fight for them for nothing!

Quick though, to talk about what Daddy did or didn't do and anytime you were a mama was when you had help. You were better off having abortions or just having your tubes tied, being done with that whole wanting to be a mother thing. Something you clearly weren't cut out for. You aren't a mother, ain't ever been a mother, nor will you ever be a mother! That's just how I feel about it, "situation!" So, the next time you want to open your mouth against me, speaking blasphemy, look into the mirror, Ms. I'll Birth You A Nation! ...Fuck! Shut down the program again. Yeah, they've managed to kill the yard.

We haven't been out in days. Today we were supposed to go out but it was some ruckus going on the lower yard. It was said to be a 3 on 1, then it was said it was 15 people involved. I guess by tonight we'll know what the actual deal was. It's not even summer yet (SMH). It's only the end of April. Sunday will be the 1st. It will be an interesting summer this year for sure. A lot of young dudes are coming here directly from the county jail, after a brief pitstop at a reception center. So you can best believe a lot of shenanigans went on in the L.A. County Jail. Some shit just catches up to you when you've been D.M.T.! And your activities went viral, especially the Mickey shit. The thing is, sometimes when you engage in shenanigan type activities they'll come back and haunt you in the worst way. Usually, shit that happens in the L.A. County Jail though, stays in the L.A. County Jail. It has nothing to do with yard life. Based on being 2 separate entities, the county is the county, the pen is the pen.

    However, your shenanigans can be so extra'ed out (over the top) that dudes are going to want to press play on you and holler at your boots (attack you) as soon as you cross paths again. Some shit can be overlooked and let go of, some can't. So you really have to be mindful always of your activities, especially if it affected your tribe b'cuz then you'll have to no doubt answer to your tribe for your indiscretions and trust Autobots will play a major role in that outcome. You will be pulled up on by the homies about the Gilligan shit that transpired. To feel otherwise is a misoverstanding and you're in a false sense of security! Dude, it's always a 360 prolonged inevitability. You're not always going to be around those same individuals that partook in or condoned your activity. Fact!

    This isn't something I've heard, it's something I've seen with my own 2 eyes. The politics get real, and real serious on that type of shit, to the point of "ball" being played or you're being whupped off the yard. The verdict was in and you've been voted off the island. Like I've stressed, it's fun and games until someone gets fly (retaliate)! My whole thing is, overstand the game you're playing comes with a cost like anything that's hazardous to your health. At the same time, if you overstand and still shoot your shot, so be it. To each his own! That's your choice to play at your own risk. You will answer though, to somebody. You're never above being pulled up on. Real talk! Oh yeah, it's real in the maze. I've preached this same sermon to many young homies I've seen on this path of bad behavior and letting them know the activities they're engaging in isn't cool. "I'm good, O.G. I know what's up!" (SMH) Yeah, until you're not good! Not just my young homies but young Crip homies, young civilians and young Damu homies that I've took a liking to at one time or another, not wanting to see them crash like a NASCAR! Now though, it's like young dudes aren't trying to hear what you're talking about. They're suffering from that "You can't tell me shit" syndrome. You're absolutely right too. I can't tell you shit! But as an older homie I can advise you. Whether you accept it or not, that's on you. But I've done my due diligence, making an attempt.

But just based on, though, my being not just an older homie but an older homie with good intentions, I'd make that attempt. I remember how when good older homies would get at me with sound advice when I was younger and on the yard at Old Folsom, Calipat and Salinas Valley in the early to late 90's, so I'm wired that way. Not just my older homies pulled up on me, but older homies from all over (from L.A. to the Bay). You had a lot of good older homies back then unlike today, with trying to steer young homies in the wrong direction or being taught and shown the wrong direction by bad dudes who could care less as long as it served their narrative or what they had going on on the yard. What I was taught and

## FEELING SOME TYPE OF WAY—SODO AUSTIN

have been taught, I've maintained it and that's why I'll make that attempt to pull up...

## Chapter 4

### "Come To The Turf"

"Come to the turf" is when you have a homie outside of the set you've built a bond and connection with from another set and you want him to "pull up" or "slide" through with you to the set to hang out with you and the homies. It's going to come a time when a dude you're fucking with on a daily that's not from the "set" is going to ask you to come to their set with them to hang out and vice versa, whether to hang out with his homies or your homies, or to just pull up or slide through momentarily, then do it moving. "Yeah homie, come through...pull up!" If it's on some hang out shit, he wants his homies to meet and know you and fuck with you to, and again vice versa. But normally when dudes do that it's all gravity b'cuz y'all fuck with each other like that and that's what it is, and it's going to be respected or so you think b'cuz a niggah's asking or you're asking for him to come or pull up. As with anything though, shit can and do go crooked too. It can be a dude asking you to come to his set or pull up and he don't got it like that.

Homies that do are going to be looking at him like, "Who the fuck this niggah think he is bringing niggahs to the turf?" Feeling some type of way. It's going to get Mickey and he'll find himself stripped the fuck out, butt ass naked b'cuz a "turned up" (active and aggressive) homie decided to run dude and run his pockets, not only dude that was brought but the homie that brought him is going to get ran too, him and his pockets. You know how homies get down. Homies trip. Not just in my turf but in every niggah's turf. I bet you're nodding your head right now, like yup...yup! When you asking a niggah you fuck with to come to the turf with you, you have to know your position. On the flip side of that, he shouldn't be all willy nilly trying to push, not knowing what he's pushing into. That's just being real and that's based on the homie might've put extras on it, as far as his status as to who he was in the turf. This niggah could be a straight buster in the homies' eyes and here you come, pulling up with this dude, like it's gravity (good). (SMH)

 Abso-lutely not, it's not good! Yeah, homies fuck with him, indeed they do, but he's not a factor. They don't fuck with him like that though. He's just a homie. He come and hang out, but not with or around homies that are "gang-gang" (active homies, everything about the turf homie). Every homie don't mess with him, certain homies do, the gang-gang homies see 'em and don't see 'em. Every turf has these type of homies from the turf, "non-factors" but their homies. So someone will definitely take issue with him just up and bringing another niggah to the turf, an unfamiliar face let alone trying to bring him on the block to hang out, a block that he's barely able to come on and hang out himself. (SMH)

 Truth be told, he's only hanging out b'cuz of the few homies that do mess with him and half ass got a little love for him and for the love and respect they have as gang-gang homies from the rest of the homies, hanging where y'all hanging. It's not a given, it's about what they're about, so homies aren't tripping off of you like that, hanging out but that doesn't give you a "pass" or the "green light" to be pulling up with niggahs. You're just recognoticed as a face that's not known for putting in work or being

## FEELING SOME TYPE OF WAY—SODO AUSTIN

gang-gang, just a face that's around. Shit, keeping it all the way hunnid, it's homies that claim the turf that won't come to the block where the active and aggressive homies are, on none of the blocks where the active and aggressive homies are.

They'll stay or be on the outskirts, on less known or active blocks. Away from the activities. Active blocks anything is subject to happen outside of homies squabbling up with each other, enemigo might pull up trying to put some work in. Niggahs ain't about that life, ain't trying to be around that life. Suuuper! When you go to another homie's turf, you have to be mindful, always mindful of a niggah's homies tripping, being on that frequency! Even if they don't trip, don't think they won't act like they won't. It's what niggahs do, your homies and the next niggah's homies too. Always keep that in the back of your mind, real talk. B'cuz it does happen and will happen, even if a dude is with a reputable niggah...

Any other thought is a niggah having a false sense of security and a mis-overstanding. It'll be a niggah homie on some shenanigans or just want to see what type of niggah the homie got in the turf with him! Seeing if he's actually a Gilligan or if he's gang-gang, it's just what niggahs do. Sometimes though, the homie is a "reputable." Checking ain't cheating, a niggah trying to see, but for the most part, if a homie that's reputable have a dude in the turf he's gang-gang from where he's from, knowing the homie. Just knowing the homie fuck with strictly gang-gang dudes and not busters. Homie(s) will still want to just test a dude's hand to see how he react or respond to a niggah getting at him, seeing if he's going to fold or get "marked out." It could be a good thing or a bad thing, who's to say? But shit, if you're feeling some type of way about the homie getting at you a certain type of way, the homie who brought you can be like, "Shit, cuz gon and get down with the homie, ain't nobody gon jump in, on the set! It's just a head up squabble."

Say though, you do get down with a niggah's homie and you're "mixin 'em up" (beating him up), putting suuuper tips (hands) on him, homies not feeling it, but it is what it is, they're not going to jump in though, based on who a niggah in the turf with. On the flip side of that though, the homie might be in his "feels" (feelings) b'cuz he got mixed and wants to take it somewhere else, which niggahs do...as we know. Everyone isn't into taking "L's," not being able to accept being served, let alone in front of other homies and homegirls, and being known for having hands too, got clowned though. But he know he can't b'cuz at the end of the day the homie asked for that and got ran. He got what he wanted... that "fade." From that day on and you're in the turf, the homie's going to be looking for a reason to get at you, for sure he's salty and working with feelings.

Don't be hanging out late night without the homie who brought you to the turf or find yourself having to take a piss in an alley or on the side of a house/apartment building. You'll fuck around and come up "bagged." Bloom! Bloom! Bloom! Bloom! I'm just saying. Riddle me this though. Who's going to say something, even if they (homies) know who put that down? Not even the homie who brought you is going to say something. Just be mindful. If a niggah was found slumped in the next niggah's turf and was brought by the next niggah, no one's going to lose any sleep over

## FEELING SOME TYPE OF WAY—SODO AUSTIN

it, nor going to trip on it, it's just a wrap, dunzo deal. That's just the reality of what could happen when a niggah asks you to come to the turf and you find yourself being a regular face, especially if you and the homies get along and it's all gravity. Sometimes other dudes' turfs become a second home.

You're suuuper comfortable and at ease with dude's homies and being in their turf. I can bang that! You're drinking and blowing with them, you're starting to "slang work" with them, you're starting to sex on their "turf rats," starting to jack with a few of them and you're even going on missions with them, bussing on mutual enemigos and even enemigos that aren't mutual. It's to the point when you're not in your turf you're in theirs. You gamble with them too. They fuck with you tough. Be mindful too that these aren't your homies, they'll turn on you and will turn on you just as quick as they'll turn on their own homies. You're expendable and don't have any ties except for the homie that brought you there. That's me being a bitterchild advocate. If it comes to their homie or it comes to you, who do you think they're going to ride with and sag it out with?

Why wouldn't you think though, they're not going to "ride with" or "sag it out" with their homie? Why wouldn't you think that though? You're not the homie, you're just a dude who hang in their turf and mess with them b'cuz one of their homies brought you. That's the only reason and the only reason they have love and respect for you, outside of you messing with them the way you do, to the extent you do...East Side! There's no tie, none whatsoever. Other than you're being brought to the turf by the homie.

## FEELING SOME TYPE OF WAY—SODO AUSTIN

Me personally, I've been in two or three turfs pushing with a homie that wasn't from the turf on some "come to the turf" type shit (his turf).

Though reluctant at times, but still "pushed" (went). Being faded always gave a dude that push, like "fuck it," ain't shit going to happen and if it do, I'm "heated" (carrying that .40). I'm sure we've all done that and been on that page. A dude faded always going to feel himself, going to be laxed and going to shoot his shot, regardless of what the fuck it is, let's go cuz! A faded dude's going to always gave that extra nudge with the case of the "fuck its!" Like shit...run it! A dude feeling invincible and on some I don't give a fuck type shit, especially off the "liquid," that "water," that "go-go" or a combination of gang drugs. But yeah, one of those turfs was when I was fucking with my niggah Robbie Rob from Park Village Compton Crip. He was like, "Come to the turf with your boy. I gottah handle some shit. We in and we out!" My knowing what type of dude he was and how he got down, I was comfortable with pushing with him to the Wilmington Arms, deep in them.

Going over there, it's like on some "one way in, one way out" type shit, pushing in a "swoop" (car) and they have a rep for being with the bullshit. You can easily come up missing fucking around in the "Arms." Anyway, I'm pushing around with him inside the Arms, meeting a few of his homies, even posted a couple of hours, though it wasn't the intentions, watching the dice game niggahs had cracking, while he chopped it up (talked), started drinking and blowing on some "trees." I'm drinking, blowing trees too and I'm chopping it up with his homies, a couple in particular b'cuz they were into music and rapped, so did I. We ended up spitting a few sixteens (rap bars) here and there. We were feeling each other's style and flow.

My shit always been on that "Bitterchild" shit! Everything I do as far as rapping, writing or pushing is based on my representation of Bitterchild. It's (my push) always coming from a Bitterchild perspective, mind state and mind frame. The way I think, the way I push and the way I deal with and approach everything, it's always applied to my everyday existence. Everything I spit or put to paper is going to have meaning and significance, with relevancy, my movement has substance.

I didn't do the dice game though, I just watched. I don't gamble in the next niggah's turf, barely gamble in my own. That's just not my get down or my demo. That look (situation) doesn't turn out cool, not by a long shot. Somebody is going to be feeling some type of way, especially losing their rabb (money). I just watched and tripped off how animated they were and were getting with each other. Especially the niggahs who were getting "bucked" (losing) for their rabbs, big shit talking! I'm talking greasy! (disrespectful) The niggahs doing the bucking is clowning...suuuper! Yeah, you can't be a dude bucking niggahs and clowning (SMH). You'll fuck around and get "flighted." The dude you came with won't be able to stop it b'cuz his homies are on you too quick. He wouldn't be able to react if he wanted to.

Shit, you done got fucked over, whupped out and stripped! The dude you came with is hot up under the collar and feeling some type of way. But shit, he's not going to go against his homies, he has to live and be around there. He knows he'll get politicked on, like in the pen, when it's all said and done. Yeah, it's politicking on the streets...indeed! Don't get me wrong, it's contradictory like a muthah fuckah, and I recognotice too, a niggah will go against his homies though, feeling as though niggahs ain't going to test his gang-gang, being on some disrespectful shit, not respecting his call b'cuz in his mind he knows he's a somebody from where he's from. He's not just some niggah from the turf but a niggah, so fuck that!

That call being, he brought a dude to the turf and bet not nobody fuck with him, to that extent he will be on some bullshit and on his too with his homies. Fuck who don't like it and is feeling some type of way about it, b'cuz it's a respect thing. A niggah ain't gon respect it, fuck them. But yeah, it was straight, didn't anything happen. I just posted and got faded. I went with him a few other times. I also ended up going in there without him b'cuz of my young piece McNeal I was sexing, she had people there. Her brody and her oldest sister Michelle's baby daddy Barnie is a somebody from over there, a balling ass niggah. Another instance, I was in the Avalon Gardens in L.A., but this instance it was b'cuz of a bitch I was fucking, a suuuper thick ass chocolate something, dark and thick as fuck. Baby had major major ass!

Nicki Minaj, Amber Rose or Black Chyna ain't had shit on her and this was in the late Eighties and the coochie was "gas" (good). Hips, thighs and legs was thick as fuck too. Titties were cool, she didn't have no suuuper big ones, but they were fairly decent. Face wasn't shit and she had

## FEELING SOME TYPE OF WAY—SODO AUSTIN

that Tyra Banks fo-head cracking. I met her through some of my other "hub" (Compton) niggahs. One of them had a BM that was cool with one of her homegirls, good look. Like I stressed, coochie was gas. Me and her brody was straight, I messed with a few of his homies through him, but not like that though. They were straight for the most part, most of them I'd met anyway, but it was a couple of them I had issue with who had an issue with me being over there b'cuz of where I was from.

Not because of my being an enemigo of theirs but b'cuz of who my turf was aligned with at that time, and I guess they were enemigos. This was like the late Eighties. At the end of the day though, a niggah from Long Beach Insane Crip...that part! Not from "L.A." I used to hear lil slick comments and lil sidewinder shit like: "What this niggah doing over here?" "Fuck this niggah!" "Cuz can't be coming up over there like that. So what he fucking the homegirl!" "What's up with the Hoover lover?" "Damn, cuz, why this Hoover loving ass niggah always over here!" It's always in reference to Hoover b'cuz my turf and Hoovers fucked with each other back then, through the 90's too.

The cold thing, though, a Hoover used to be up over there. Niggahs didn't say shit to him. He was my boy from Compton's baby mama brother, the one who hooked me up with ole girl I was sexing over there. It just got to be too much after a while and I was cool on dudes lil bullshit ass remarks and in general feeling some type of way. I just got at a niggah on some real shit verbally and it ended up going crooked. Needless to say, I stopped fucking around over there.

## FEELING SOME TYPE OF WAY—SODO AUSTIN

That played a part, the other part was my catching the bitch I was sexing sleep in the bed naked with one of her homies from over there. Leg out from under the covers to where you could see clearly she didn't have no panties on and her left titty was exposed. Oh yeah, I was straight, it was fun while the "funzies" lasted (having sex on call with her anywhere), please believe it. Gripping those thick dark chocolate ass hips, sexing her doggy style, seeing all that ass and those big round dark ass cheeks, jumping, shaking, wiggling and jiggling while she pushed back into a niggah as she whined up and rolled her hips and ass in a slow circular motion, looking back at me. "Bye bye, see yah later...call you if I had your number!"

It was fun laying on top of her though, with all my weight in between her thick, wide, parted legs and thighs, sexing her, feeling her underneath me, whining, rolling and rocking her hips, ass and coochie, fucking a niggah back. It was suuuper fun while it lasted, having her on top, in reverse, riding the dick, looking at all that ass and hips moving the way she moved, boy was it fun. Couldn't suck no dick, though. A niggah didn't ask me in that instance to come to the turf b'cuz I was already in the turf sexing a niggah sister. What up, Kim? It was more like come fuck with me and my homies. I knew, though, if I would've kept popping up over there I would've come up "bagged" (dead) or I would've had to bag (kill) a niggah! B'cuz it was always going to be an issue. Even though ole girl's brody used to get at his homies like, "Stall a niggah out, he's straight!" Or, "Kick back on cuz!" They still had lil shit to say. But, yeah, for the most part, it's really not a good look. To each his own though.

## FEELING SOME TYPE OF WAY—SODO AUSTIN

It's too many elements that come with going to a niggah's turf with him, or being in their turf. Too much bullshit can come into play and be in play. Not to mention that "you fucking with them, you ducking with them element," you're hit when their enemies pull up on some gang-gang shit! But yeah, it's always going to be that one niggah with the shenanigans that'll have an issue with you or is going to feel some type of way about something.

Its been instances where I've seen other homies brought dudes in the turf and you will hear a bunch of: "Who's cuz? Where cuz from?" This, that and the third from homies have a niggah pressured up. Depending on who a niggah over there with, a homie might shoot the sarcastic shit at the homies if he hear the homies inquiring about where a niggah from, like they're pressing (tripping). "You want to know so bad, pull up and get at him. I'm sure he'll tell you, he's not a buster!" One of the homies done "gas'ed" it up though, just that quick (SMH). One thing I know and can attest to, you can't be wandering off by yourself in a niggah's turf all willy-nilly (without a care in the world), especially if you haven't been over there like that and messing with the homies, and they don't really know you or feel you like that.

Don't do it and I wouldn't advise it. Not at all! B'cuz homies do trip. A dude will find himself saying, "I'm over here with such and such!" But the thing is, you're at the "Highway Center" (a store in the turf, no longer there, though), without such and such, so you could get sweated, depending on who it is that pull up on you. I've seen that look (situation) a million or so times. Some homies just don't and won't give a fuck who you

## FEELING SOME TYPE OF WAY—SODO AUSTIN

say you're messing with in the turf or where the fuck you're posted at. I've tripped before and have told a niggah to beat it! But yeah, you're just at the store, you should've come to the store with the homie as far as they were concerned, I'm just saying that's how homies getting down and getting it in.

I can safely say though, that's what it be and will come to. I've had dudes say, "Yo homie such and such told me it was straight for me to be over here!" Or, "Such and such know I'm over here!" All that's fine and well, but if you're not with them, or they aren't close by, you're opening yourself up to and for the bullshit. A homie's going to be feeling some type of way. For the most part though homie, niggahs should be skeptical about going to a dude's turf or be so quick to go. Don't get me wrong or twisted, I've ran across and came across all types of dudes in the City, in the turf and on the outskirts of the turf and didn't trip, Crips and Bloods. I don't trip on or off dudes, especially if you're not on no goofball shit and DTM (doing too much). I'm not tripping off of you, do you. Just know and respect where you are. I don't have shit to say to you, I'm going to keep it moving up the street in my swoop, blowing my blunt and banging my music...my music! I'm not bussing "nare" (no) U-turn. I mean, I get and overstand, it's how dudes built ties, rapports and relationships and want to pull up or have you pull up. I overstand dudes make relationships and create allies, dudes been doing it for years in the pen and it falls into the street once they get out, touching concrete, dudes continue fucking with each other.

## FEELING SOME TYPE OF WAY—SODO AUSTIN

By going to different turfs messing with dudes, it builds bridges and builds bonds too, lasting ones. Therefore, having a rapport and can have a dialogue if a situation comes about, never know where you might end up or be in the streets, especially if you're not one of the homies that's just turf bound and venture out. You never know where a venture might have you or take you, I get all that and I'm mindful of it. It's a good look in that sense, dudes being able to communicate and can bridge gaps. Niggahs come up "bagged" and "flighted" in another niggah's turf everyday somewhere. Not just b'cuz a niggah got caught slipping where he shouldn't have been but b'cuz he stayed in the next niggah's turf and they decided to trip on him, but b'cuz he went to the next niggah's turf, b'cuz he was asked to come and he was tripped on, period.

Again, it doesn't just have to be he went with a homie who wasn't gang-gang, that didn't have the respect like that to be just bringing a dude in the turf without being a victim himself behind it. He can be a homie that's gang-gang and it'll still happen. Don't get it confused, it just don't happen as often, but it does happen and I can bang that! It depends on the situation for the most part, b'cuz who's to say if you're not around the homie that brought you, a niggah's going to trip, or he's not, I would think, though.

If you're around or with the homie that brought you and he's a reputable, it's gravity, supposed to be. Homies shouldn't trip and if for some reason a homie tripping, you can get that head-up fade with him and nobody's going to jump. It's just you and that homie, whether he's getting whupped out or not, nobody's going to get in it and if they do, I can see a

## FEELING SOME TYPE OF WAY—SODO AUSTIN

homie tripping (the one who brought you) on some "Fuck that!" type shit, feeling like he's being disrespected, like he's not gang-gang or don't have it like that, to make that call and have it respected, depending on the homie, depending on what homie you know. I've brought a couple of homies I fucked with to the turf and had them in the spot with me on 20th and Myrtle and it was all gravity.

My niggahs respected my call and respected the fact I was gang-gang, not to trip or say anything. I've had niggahs around that weren't homies, but was from the City, same shit and they were embraced. It wasn't no shenanigans or nothing to that effect, they posted up and it was good. For the most part, my niggahs don't be with the bullshit, though some do be on the goofball shit, from time to time. That's a given, homies are homies. That's niggahs period though, with the shenanigans. Aye, it's a cold game, that's what a dude do know, cold as fuck. At times, dudes make it up as they go, or so it seems.

I've seen it go suuuper crooked with a niggah coming in the turf with a homie who wasn't gang-gang, fucked around and got his ass whupped out and got the niggahs he brought whupped out, horseplaying! Just on him being arrogant enough to be on some Gilligan ass shit like that, what was he thinking? This shit's not a game and it's not a joke, dudes have to be mindful of what the hell they're doing when they're doing it. When it's all said and done though, you should always be mindful, basically following or being led blindly. Dudes will say anything to appear or seem like somebody they aren't. Will try to convince you it's all gravity and homies ain't tripping and don't trip like that. This, that and the third, he's a gang-gang homie with big love and big respect in his turf with his homies. You're good, don't have shit to worry about (SMH). Just big popping it! You go for it, it is what it is, shoot your shot. He's going to sell it to you, especially if he feels you're kind of reluctant and not trying to push. On this last note before I park on this subject, a dude asking you to come to the next dude's turf with him and it's gravity, he's his boy, that should always be a pause off top on your part give it thought. That can go bad in so many ways. It's not his turf and those aren't his homies. He's just straight with a dude from over there, he can easily get tripped on and you're there too, so guess what? You fucking with 'em, you ducking with 'em! What you thought was going to happen? You're tripped on too, be mindful.

That's just some real shit and a game a dude really isn't trying to play...whaaat! I mean, if that's what you do, just be mindful of what you signed up for, mindful of the possibility of shit going sideways or crooked. Those aren't your homies and it's not your turf. Shit's unpredictable, like homies are going to be. Reality is something we all share. Don't nobody escape it. "Come to the turf" is being asked basically to go hang out in an unfamiliar area, with unfamiliar faces, with somebody you know and fuck with...

… FEELING SOME TYPE OF WAY—SODO AUSTIN

# Chapter 5

## "Rabbs Change Shit"

Rabbs change shit most...most definitely. Due to the element of not having them, then having them, respecting rabbs and not respecting them. Shit's going to change from both sides of the equation as I came to learn, know and overstand it to be. Just touching the little bit I was able to touch, being in the game and having an underground clothing line called Bitter Child Clothing, I was half ass messing with, I could only imagine what it would have been or could've been had I been on my shit, full throttle. Just on the level a niggah was doing it, started to change shit. As the fans became fans, the rabbs started coming little by little. I even started fucking with the homie Hobo from the turf who was actually a "cry baby" from the turf, can't recall which one. He was an up and coming rapper. I would shoot him free Bitter Child shit to promote the brand.

Other homies or people would see him in it and would pull up on me. The next thing you know, that's a little more recognition and a little more rabbs in a niggah's pocket. V.I.P. Records in the turf on PHC (Pacific Coast Highway) and King supported my Bitterchild push and movement too. They sold my T-shirts and hoodies, I dealt with the owner Calvin and his daughter Tasha. You already know what came with those mutha fuckin haters (SMH)...Whaaat! Somebody told them, the owners, they were messing with a dope dealer and a gang banger. There went the relationship, just like that! (SMH) Just as quick as the relationship started, it ended. We made a few rabbs together, though, before it went Bluey-

## FEELING SOME TYPE OF WAY—SODO AUSTIN

Bluey (all bad). Some weirdo hated on me and wasn't trying to see me eating (getting rabbs) with V.I.P.

But yeah, shit changes from both sides of the coin, believe it, for the better or for the worse. Now you have a mutha fucka switching up on you or saying you've switched up on them (SMH). Those you thought were with you, for you and fucking with you, come to find out that wasn't the case. Straight Gilligan ass mutha fuckas at the end of the day. Rabbs will expose people for who they really are and what they're really about, and how they really feel about a dude while they're feeling some type of way. You will find out just how much they were with you, for you and fucking with you, to what extent. What your relationship was really based on, realness or fakeness. Life has a bunch of funny ass ways and a cold way of exposing them, yes...sir! And I can bang that! Showing you just how a mutha fucka will switch up on you, like an audible, b'cuz you're having them (rabbs), some mutha fuckas will have a nerve to try and make you feel guilty for getting what you got and having what you have, like you're doing them wrong or something. Imagine that, though (SMH). Allah bless the child who has his mutha fucking own! That's some real shit at its finest. That adage wasn't said for nothing. Get a bar! Get your mind around it.

Dudes will all of a sudden be feeling some type of way and working with F and E's, out of the grey, and feeling like you owe them something. But they weren't on the block "nan" (no) night or day with a niggah, slanging nan sack or nan piece of work (dope), ain't ran from nan police, damn sure ain't hopped over nan gate, climbed over nan fence. If you don't knock it the fuck off! Now I get the meaning of "more rabbs, more problems!" It come with problems, drama and headaches, suuuper! I can bang that! It's as if a mutha fucka just start losing his God damn mind. Dudes start looking at you different and fucking with you different as if you're changing, yet you're the same niggah you've always been.

Before you were getting rabbs and were broke, it was all gravity and to the good. You were on the same playing field as they were. On some just getting by type shit, working a sack, trying to flip it! But basically end up just getting your "re-up" rabbs back, not really growing or making no headway. It's the same ole shit, b'cuz a dude has to eat, you're buying trees, buying drink and probably tricking off a few rabbs fucking with a turf rat (loose and fast female). You're doing everything but stacking, real talk. You can't grow or get anywhere with that mindset, absolutely not. Especially trying to stack but fucking off on a turf rat. They did say, "You can lose rabbs chasing a bitch, but you can't lose a bitch chasing rabbs." Cold sentiment, huh? That's always a thought to be mindful of for those that overstand that, K.T.S.E.! It's a whole lot of meaning in that sentiment being said. Some niggahs are just on spending every rabb they're encouraged to stack, as if that rainy day isn't going to exist.

Going to need it and not going to have it, bad look. You're basically fucking off on a daily, knowing the get down, being all about the now, that instant gratification that rabbs bring for that time being. Big fun, big drink, big blowing, getting big pussy. Til it's all gone and you're scrambling again, trying to make it add up and make sense, not getting nowhere moving like that. Nah, can't forget about the few rabbs a niggah fuck off fucking with turf rats, getting rooms (motel rooms). Sometimes dudes get the room and she ain't giving up the coochie but acted like she was. It ended up being, "Come on, let's just lay here, let's cuddle." I've kicked bitches out of the room for less, horseplaying! I didn't get the room to lay there and cuddle. Bitch, if you don't knock it off! You're not even a niggah's bitch, you have no room to be playing games.

Dudes stay fucking off on rooms, trying to sex on something, something new or something old. Don't let it be a female you've been trying to hump on for a cool minute and all of a sudden she's interested b'cuz she hears you're getting rabbs. Its big action jumping off, bitch is touchy feely, acting silly and being playful, laughing at your corny ass jokes (SMH). Yeah, you're going to take advantage of the situation. Why not? She's only trying to mess with you, being on some thirsty shit. I'm going to need my issue (sex). Yeah, you get something out of me, you're sucking and fucking! Every time I feel I'm about to "blow her mouth up," I'm going to pull out until I'm ready to buss, then when I do, I'm bussing in her mouth and on her mouth.

Then she's going to be fucking until I can't buss no more and the coochie is dry as fuck and all sexed out...and sore. Her shits going to hurt just to touch it. It's going to hurt catching a breeze between her legs. Yeah, jokes on her b'cuz a niggah cool on her. The curiosity isn't there any longer. Half the time the sex isn't what a niggah expected. At the end of the day, they're good for a couple of rabbs to walk away with, fucking with

## FEELING SOME TYPE OF WAY—SODO AUSTIN

me. Literally a couple of rabbs. My couple is like a hot fifteen or twenty, and they can take what we didn't drink up or blow. Shit, all that sucking and fucking, you deserve it. Neck aching, coochie sore, yeah, you put in work and got work put in on you. I can see you wit that. Don't get at me though, I'll get at you, I know where to pull up on you at. Moving along though, you recognotice how as long as you don't have shit and don't have shit in motion, dudes are content and cool with you in that state. As far as they're concerned, you're on the same page, neither of you has shit. You ain't got shit, they ain't got shit! And y'all are basically copping the same amount of work. Not growing, steady copping quarter piece after quarter piece. He's not growing and not trying to see you grow either. Fuck it, y'all can stay stagnated together.

    Oh trust, niggah's are straight with you being on that page. Even the niggahs you're in traffic with on a daily, hustling with...it's all gravity. The minute you start seeing some rabbs, here come the bullshit and shenanigans. Dudes start being with the funnies, acting all weird around you and distant at times. New behavior, none of this was going on though, when you were broke as fuck and just getting by. Yeah, big laughs, big clowning and the atmosphere was different. Shit got serious and real, but all of a sudden. Where was this shit at earlier? Riddle me that! Just out of the grey niggahs changing their movement around you differently and how they function with you. Why the sudden change though? A niggah didn't change, it's the same ole three step. They're acting like you're the niggah who changed and started acting funny, being on some janky shit! B'cuz

## FEELING SOME TYPE OF WAY—SODO AUSTIN

you got your weight up and leveled up! They're the mutha fuckas who changed, it ain't you (SMH).

All you did was change your dress code, got a little flyer, went from smoking "struggle" (stress) to "gas" (high quality weed). Went from brandy to "yac" (cognac), any of them. Went from a "bucket" (hooptie car) to a swoop sitting on hunnid spokes (Dayton wire wheels) with major beat in it, still messing with the same dudes and sexing the same type of bitches, turf rats! The individual hasn't changed. The material shit should never change a dude, though for some it does. But that's just a niggah who's not used to having shit and don't know how to act when he touches a little bit of rabbs. Those are the dudes that find themselves being a homie's "come up" (robbery victim). It's a known fact, a lot of dudes "come up" off their homies. You do have these few homies that do run homies' pockets (rob them), stripping them out...let me get that! Straight eating and living off stripping homies out, strictly come up off homies. Yeah, my old boy "I.C." know a thing or two about that, homies stripped him out (SMH). Homies know who to get at though, and who not to. Every niggah approached with that isn't accepting it. Homies know who'll play ball and who won't.

Me and a homie at the time (I.C.) had a spot (dope house). A "G" homie popped up talking about he heard homies "fresh out" could come through and get some work. It was the "G" homie (Big Bouncer). We looked out for homie, he comes back on some Gilligan shit, talking about he had to throw it before the police got up on him, un-huh (SMH). But can he get something else, not knowing the homie's smoking like a chimney and a broke stove combined. The homie had the audacity to come back asking for something else. He wasn't trying to spend, he was just trying to come up on some free shit to smoke on. Told him wasn't nothing happening and to do it moving, had nothing for him. He was no doubt feeling some type of way and working with F and E's.

Didn't care about none of that. Niggahs ah lay yo big ass out! He bounced but what he was doing was hanging out down the street from the spot on "2-1" and Myrtle. He was down there trying to "short stop" and get his "jack on" (rob customers), anybody the hit the block on foot, coming to the spot, he was on them. "Clines" (customers) were telling us what the homie was doing down there. Me and the homie just decided to slide him a little something so he could get the fuck on and off the block before it got took to another level.

Keeping it a hunnid, I was feeling some type of way and had started working with F and E's on some "fuck this niggah" type shit, he's not fucking with no buster, I'm gang-gang with all the festivities. Based on being who you were, niggahs looked out for you...you came back... looked out for you again. You tried coming back a third time, then was told niggahs done all they were going to do. Then you go somewhere else with it, trying to take food out of niggahs' mouths. Dudes got bills, got kids, got a situationship, got habits (trees, water and drink). Plus I had a lightweight "tricking bill" (motel rooms, hair or nails here and there, maybe a couple of rabbs to look out). That was only with bitches I was sexing on a "reggo" (regular) on some homie-lover-friend type shit.

## FEELING SOME TYPE OF WAY—SODO AUSTIN

    The random turf rats didn't have shit coming, for the most part, but some dick and a hard mutha fuckin time. You might get left with the rest of what we didn't kill (finish), and that was depending on if you sucked some "bomb" (good) dick and you had a decent sex game. Other than that, it might of been b'cuz I had you sucking for forty-five minutes or so after I smoked a stick (sherm stick) or I fucked until I couldn't buss no more and shit was dry and sore. Back to what I was saying, though, about the sudden change in dudes' behavior towards a niggah. They changed. They started moving around a niggah differently, they started fucking with a niggah differently, like you're the one who did the changing.

    You're still messing with them, you're still around them, you're not on no "flossing" (high signing) type shit, trying to clown niggahs or act brand new, it's the same you you've been. Ain't shit changed with you, it's all them and whatever it is they're on, for whatever reason they're on it. Being on that shit though, they'll make a niggah get brand new, have a niggah change and switch up! Not b'cuz that's what a niggah wanted to do, but b'cuz they gave a niggah no choice. It's crazy though, we're supposed to be niggahs at the end of the day. I'm not doing anything you can't do or having anything you can't have. A dude might of decided to get on his "grown niggah tip" and level up! Stack and say I'm over that Gilligan shit, I'm chasing rabbs. Chasing rabbs, trying to make it make sense and add the fuck up, 86'ing that other shit, leaving that for the birds!

    Leave it for the niggahs that's not trying to see themselves with it and content with just getting by. Just living day to day, just to buy

## FEELING SOME TYPE OF WAY—SODO AUSTIN

something to drink or whatever their recreational drug of choice is. Some dudes are "straight" (OK) with that. Like those dudes that are cool with running to the county building getting "GR" (general relief). Same dudes that are just speaking on the next dude and what the next dude doing or isn't doing wit his. Technically that shouldn't concern you, that's just a dude worrying too much about the wrong thing. But you want to feel some type of way and make me feel some type of way, b'cuz a dude is doing and being him...not you! What am I doing you can't do? Riddle me that. There's nothing stopping you but air and opportunity. Yeah, "air and opportunity," that's it that's all. I mean, damn, how long is a dude supposed to be stagnated and stuck at the same level? At what point is it a'ight to grow?

I saw firsthand how rabbs change shit with dudes, having them think once they have it they're above politics or above being touched, or can just buy niggahs and buy their loyalty. Not just that, but buy their self "passes" (get out of trouble free pass) when they do Mickey shit or are caught up in Mickey shit. Dudes that have rabbs for some reason or another do some snitching, then they try to toss niggahs rabbs and sacks, putting them on. Usually, the niggahs that "bite" and play ball are the Thirsty McGurts (dudes accepting whatever and look the other way) Then "Ole Thirsty" trying to find a way to justify the whole situation. There is no justifying shit a snitch niggah brought you b'cuz he knew you could be bought and he knew he could afford you.

## FEELING SOME TYPE OF WAY—SODO AUSTIN

That's all types of crazy, feeding off negative energy. I guess some niggahs do know they can buy passes when they're getting rabbs. It can't buy everything or anybody, that's for certain. You can't buy off that dude who's dead set on bagging your telling ass...and I can bang that! That's just crazy as fuck to me, how dudes will take work and rabbs from a snitch who has it and give them that pass (SMH). Allowing them to continue to hang out and function in the turf, openly messing with this dude like he never snitched or that never existed. If you don't knock it off. Dudes don't have no values or morals nowadays. I guess it's all the gang drugs. It's not just that dudes are just sellouts. That's been going on way before the gang drugs. Dudes are selling their souls for jelly rolls, fuck a value, fuck a moral. What do you have for a niggah? They say rabbs make a difference, but don't make you different. Something to ponder, huh? And get your mind around. It's just crazy to me too how when you start having rabbs, dudes jump right to the bullshit. "You changed, you acting funny, you ain't the same niggah!" ..."You on some bullshit, you done got too good to fuck wit niggahs!" Or it's: "Sup, baller baller!" Damn, when did a niggah change his name? I didn't know I changed my shit! All of a sudden, I went from "Such and Such" to "Baller Baller!" Dudes are just going to give you a name huh? I ain't ever said my name was Baller Baller. When did I become a baller though? (SMH)

Plotting on a niggah's downfall! I ain't got no more than the next dude on his grind. Not me per se I'm speaking on, but on behalf of dudes in general. Those who can identify with those sentiments and can relate. Being better than niggahs, since when a niggah still fucking with niggahs and being around. If a niggah felt like that, I'm sure his "demo" would reflect just that! He wouldn't be around as much, he'll just slide through or pull up for a hot second and he's out. Never parking, will just sit in the street holding up traffic, long enough to say a few words, then he's pulling off. That'll be his existence and what he'll be known for. Again, since when? That to me is just some shit. The next dude's going through issues he has. He's working with issues that ain't got shit to do with you, he's feeling some type of way.

    The reality of it, it's b'cuz he knows he's on some Gilligan shit, but doesn't know how to approach the situation, so that's his way of lashing out. That shit is weird. It's not just him, it's the next dude too, feeling some type of way b'cuz that's what he want to do. He always have something slick coming out of his mouth...he can't see a dude and not say shit (SMH). "Here come the baller baller!" ..."Let a niggah hold something homie!" ..."Put a niggah on homie!" ..."I see you, I see you!" (SMH) I mean, what's a niggah's motivation? Riddle me that one!

    Keep it a hunnid, that's a dude being on some suuuper haterism, homie or not! What's the hate for? A dude ain't got shit better to do than to keep being with the shenanigans? A dude on the block like you, doing what you're doing and gang gang. The cold thing about it, you're hating and a dude probably don't have nothing near or close to what niggahs might think he has. Illusions are a mutha fucka. We all know illusions of truth wear a mask of deception well. Shit, getting the wrong idea is on the next dude, if he got that illusion. It wasn't put out there purposely, a dude's just doing and being him, making it make sense for him. A lot of times

## FEELING SOME TYPE OF WAY—SODO AUSTIN

dudes don't be having what dudes think they have, but damn homie...you're worrying too much about the wrong shit. Get you some business.

It's hard to get a read on dudes. What ain't hard to read though, is dudes change way before you do. They don't give you a chance to change, if that's what he was going to do, it's like dudes turn the bullshit dial up to a hunnid (SMH). First thing out their mouth, "That niggah thank he all that...he thank he the shit!" Damn! Hate...hate...hate! According to who though? Where did those words come from? Who said them? When you have rabbs, granted it does change a lot in a dude's space, as far as what it brings, what it attracts and what it breeds. It brings hate...it brings jealousy...it brings envy...it brings thirsty bitches and niggahs, and breeds them all. Having rabbs brings shit to you and problems you never had to deal with before.

You'll find out how shit around you change first. The change will come subtle. It could be recognoticed, depending on the elements and the big captured moment. I guess from knowing what I know, I can overstand the dynamics and why dudes who get rabbs distance themselves and be on the shit they're on most of the time. I get why they push. It affects dudes and keeping it a hunnid, some niggahs that don't have it do deserve it and some that don't have it don't deserve it. Rabbs make a difference clearly, but don't make you different. At least in my mind. Dudes should always be mindful of that, I get it. The dudes that have it do the wrong things with it a lot of the times b'cuz they don't respect it. It came easy. The dudes that don't have it wish they had it to do anything with, based on knowing they're going to make it make sense. The shit's going to add up and it's going to count. Not saying it's not going to come with or have its share of issues, issues are just a part of it. How can there be joy without pain? All actuality, rabbs do change shit, the way dudes dress, the way they look, the way he lives and what he blows, going from struggle to "Kush," what he drives and in some cases the type of bitch he's pulling up on. We're not talking about the little turf rat or the homie-lover-friend bitches, hump on when they're getting rabbs. Neither one of them aren't the one you really mess with. Those are just the ones you "hump on" in traffic, which is where you keep those relationships, in traffic.

    They're not the one you go home to or play house with, calling them "wifey." Nah-uh, they're just something to do for funzies and buss nuts in. Even the type of dudes a niggah fuck with outside off his homies in the turf. You'll find out just how thirsty homies get and can be when they're on their thirsty shit...being thirst balls (SMH). Dudes see you in a whole different light and way for some reason or another. When you start looking like you're getting rabbs, they'll just take it as if you're flossing or "stunting" on them b'cuz you're driving something fly and they aren't. I don't even get how they get to that conclusion or how their mental even get there (SMH). It boggles my mind, its just "burnt out" (crazy).

    I'm not even going to begin to try to overstand it or figure it out. That's just too much thinking for me. A niggah will be going around in circles trying to grasp that. They're not feeling your drinking Hennessey, your dress code changing, you're wearing jewels, you're blowing "Kush," you have rabbs in your pocket. You have a whole different demeanor

## FEELING SOME TYPE OF WAY—SODO AUSTIN

about yourself, that confidence is being reflected and you're appearing to be more at ease in your space. None of that is being felt, not at all. Having rabbs will change the narrative and dynamics in a real way, whether you want shit to change or not. You basically don't have any control over it. Change is inevitable, being able to do shit you weren't able to before, going to spots you weren't able to before.

Sexing bitches you weren't able to before, being around dudes you weren't able to be around before, b'cuz these dudes are strictly on their rabbs tip. If you're not on yours, you're not going to be in their space, all that changed. You will find yourself attracting all types of shit, that's changed too. One thing though, I came to overstand is how rabbs attract rabbs. When you're having them or are getting it, you attract other dudes that have it or are getting it. You'll start fucking with each other, moving in the same circles, turning each other on to different plays (ways of getting rabbs...plugs, etc.). You'll be networking with each other, all that's changed. It's not a bad thing, it's growth. But yeah, you're not going to see too many dudes with it fucking with dudes without it. It doesn't really mix, based on.

If they do, it's only to an extent, either they're serving a purpose or is being fed. It's not so much as dudes feeling or thinking he's better than a mutha fucka, they just know how it breeds envy and how a mutha fucka will get on some thirsty shit, making him have to show a niggah rabbs didn't make him soft, he's still gang gang... forcing his hand. Some dudes do though, turn soft once they start having it (SMH), start allowing shit they wouldn't have ever allowed before they were having it. Not all, though, turn soft. A niggah was gang gang before the rabbs and will continue to be gang gang. As soon as a dude try to shoot his shot he's going to find himself in a wreck. ...Whaaat! Flag on the homie! Especially a dude's homie. They'll be the first to try to shoot their shot. Like I'd stressed, they know who to test the waters with and who not to.

If they know or think it's going to "go up" (get violent) fucking with you, they're going to rethink the play. Dudes prey on easy shit, they're not fucking with anything that's going to be met by resistance. I can't lie, it will have you, well, can have you on some arrogant shit. I can see it, done seen it, it was me before. I don't think it's intentional or was intended. A bitch complimented me on an all royal blue leather jacket I was wearing at a party one of my female cuzzos threw (not blood related). I admit, it was an eye catcher, it was dope. As soon as I stepped in the door, looks, mutha fuckas were on it. A lil bitch was like, "Ooh, I like your jacket, it look good on you!" I just looked at her and said, "I know, I like it too, that's why I bought it!" I walked off, not before getting another eyeful of her. She shook her head, trying to save face, having the last word she was on some, "I was just complimenting your jacket, niggah, damn!" I don't even know why I went there with her, besides, being in my F and E's b'cuz one of my homie-lover-friends was up in the spot (SMH), the bitch didn't come with me. You never take sand to the beach. She came with one of my blood relatives. Which was crazy, knowing I would pull up. Not going to be able to do shit or pull up on nothing b'cuz she's going to be trying to be near me, cock blocking.

## FEELING SOME TYPE OF WAY—SODO AUSTIN

  I wouldn't be leaving there with nan bitch! Not if she had anything to do with it. She wasn't even my bitch, a niggah had a situationship and kids at home on the North Side. Like I said, homie-lover-friend, slide through, blow, sip on something, fuck and up out of there. I'd hit her phone, "Aye, I'm on my way!" Any time of night, it was always gravity. Bitch just got too attached. I guess, with ole girl, I was on some: "Yeah, bitch, you look good and all that, but you ain't shit!" You know how bitches be sizing dudes up, trying to see what a niggah working with? I'm not talking about a niggah's dick. I'm talking about what type of rabbs a niggah's working with, being pocket checked. Typical bitch knows she looks good and stay trying to find a sucker to take care of her pretty ass. Straight play on her looks too, trying to be all she can be and get all she can get. You attract those type of bitches, it's automatic, they come automatic.

  As do haters, comes with the territory. Change will happen, that's just what it is, whether you choose to embrace it or not, but don't let the change change you. Always overstand it doesn't make you better or above somebody, or they're beneath you, b'cuz you're on (have it) and they aren't. It don't make them less than b'cuz they're not on (not having it), it's not their time. However, we all get a turn at some point though. But yeah, "Rabbs Change Shit!" That's just what the frequency is, homie...

# Chapter 6

### "Going Against The Grain"

Going against the grain, my dude, it's just what it is, going against the grain. Basically, going against what you know you shouldn't be going against when it comes to the rules, codes and politics of the turf. Going against a homie you're tight with for a homie you just fuck with and are straight with. Going against a "call" made by a "G" homie, not just any G homie but a reputable G homie that has and carry suuuper weight in the turf. Being gang gang. Going against the grain can have suuuper consequences. It's basically a dude shooting his shot against all odds, on some Mickey shit. Testing a situation or testing a mutha fucka's patience, seeing just how far you can go or push limits before something will happen...can happen (SMH). Going against the grain isn't for everyone, everyone isn't built like that. Me personally, I've always been a fan of going against the grain, standing on my own beliefs, values and principles, whether I believed fat meat was greasy or not.

But, oh yeah homie, it's greasy as a mutha fucka. Church's Chicken grease don't have shit on going against the grain grease when it's Mickey! I learned the hard way on more than a few occasions, just doing and being me. Overstanding it can be a good thing or a bad thing, depending on what a niggah's on. "The push" or "the cause." It can be a bigger captured moment though, with consequences. It is what it is though. I have a younger homie from the turf that I knew since he was like around seven or eight years old. I hadn't seen him for like twelve or thirteen years, at least.

## FEELING SOME TYPE OF WAY—SODO AUSTIN

I went to the "Y" (Y.A), then got out, didn't see him the few months I was out, then I ended up going to the pen, catching like fourteen years and eight months. I heard he was in a wheelchair. I heard somewhat of the circumstances that surrounded the "get down" but you know how that goes. Yup, it was Mickey!

    To my overstanding, lil homie went to the "Y," came home on suuuper swole and was on some extra'ed out shit with the whole: "Can't nobody tell me shit! I'm gang gang!" This is me, this is what it is, it's my push, fuck this! Fuck that! Fuck these niggahs! Fuck that niggah! This, that and the third. The homie was turned up, his attitude was: "Don't nobody like it, fuck them too!" A worst case of the fuck its! During this time he was off the streets, the turf and the enemigos were on a peace treaty, basically a ceasefire. Niggahs fell back. Niggahs were still getting rushed and were lining up, still catching fades too.

    From what I was told, the homie wasn't feeling the ceasefire, not at all and was feeling some type of way. I can overstand his feeling though, based on his cuzzo getting bagged by enemigo and the same ones it was a ceasefire with! I think I would've been in the same predicament the young homie was in, being in that mutha fuckin' wheelchair, just based on. I wouldn't have been trying to hear shit nan mutha fucka was talking about...no bueno! Fuck that! I also heard too though, he had action at getting out of the chair, but he gave up on walking. That part right there! I wouldn't have been able to do it. I would've been trying to walk again. A "G" homie from what the streets was saying got at young homie on some,

## FEELING SOME TYPE OF WAY—SODO AUSTIN

"Cuz, it's ceasefire we're not doing that, everything else though, we can press play on, we're not playing ball!" Young homie got at the "G" homie who's known for playing ball on some sideways shit, like he wanted to squabble up with him.

Fucked around and it was bluey bluey, found himself shot and sitting in a wheelchair...horseplaying for sure! His bad! It was a Mickey situation for the homie. But yeah, sometimes you have to know when to pick your battles and fall back. Clearly the G homie was the wrong niggah to be fucking with (SMH). That's just keeping it one hunnid with you. That's a classic case of when going against the grain went wrong and it went viral. It was on some, "You gon respect my gang gang and respect my call or else!" Young homie was on, "I lost my mutha fuckin cuzzo, I'm with the or else!" I mean shit, at the end of the day, I can't knock either homie for what they were on, for what and as it was, me just being and playing bitterchild advocate (devil's advocate). That bad look was imminent and knocking at a dude's door.

It's a lot of that going on in dudes' turfs, homies going against the grain. Some just b'cuz, some to prove a point, some b'cuz they felt it was the right thing to do not being an Autobot and fuck who's feeling some type of way about it! That was my basic attitude about the going against the grain thing. If it's deemed necessary I'm pressing play on it, period. Don't agree or are feeling some type of way about my choice, fuck it, that's my energy. According to a couple of homies, I'm going against the grain now b'cuz it's felt I shouldn't have wrote "A Bitter child State Of Mind" and now I'm writing this one (SMH). Feeling I'm waking dudes'

## FEELING SOME TYPE OF WAY—SODO AUSTIN

game up, which I shouldn't be and I should leave them asleep...flag on the play! If I can wake a niggah's game up, especially young homies, why not? If he's receptive. If he can learn from the next niggah's mistakes, why not?

I think my most memorable one though, was when my homies, dudes I ran with were feeling some type of way about another homie. It was a homie I kind of half-assed had love for b'cuz we grew up together, on some sandbox type shit (adolescence). Homies wanted to bang him over some stupid shit. The homie wasn't a snitch. Had that been the case, I would've personally had a hand in it, and I can bang that! I couldn't see it happening though, and voiced my feelings on the matter. What the homies were tripping off of the homie for didn't warrant him being "bagged." Not by a long shot. I defended the homie and went to bat for him. The homies weren't feeling it and wasn't feeling me at that point. But at the end of the day, I'm like fuck it! B'cuz that was some bullshit that was going on, as far as what was being tripped on (SMH).

As I'd stressed, had it been on some snitching type shit, even on some serious Mickey shit, he was getting voted off the island and had to go, "bluey bluey!" It just didn't warrant that and I stood firm on it. Did I take a chance of being turned on or tripped on? Indeed! But I was willing to take that ride! Did I take a chance of being bagged myself? Indeed I was, knowing my homies. I felt though, I had to go against the grain on that b'cuz it was Mickey and homies were trying to play ball on a good homie. Anything else would've been a misoverstanding that just didn't sit right with me. Another situation where I had to go against the grain was

## FEELING SOME TYPE OF WAY—SODO AUSTIN

when the homies wanted me to "jack" (rob) my "plug" (connect)...that was out! You niggahs wasn't about to fuck what I had going on, up, or take food off my plate being on some thirsty shit! I was messing with a "Paisa" who I had "got in" (befriended) with on a fluke (by chance), not on no suuuper weight or nothing, just on some lil shit.

Nah, I'm not going to have you believe I was getting big "pigeons" (keys/kilos) and pounds from him, not at all, not by a long shot. I was only copping nine "zips" (ounces), but as our relationship progressed and the trust developed and was up, he started fronting me nine zips on top of the nine I was already copping from him and a pound of some fire ass trees he shot me for three twenty-five. He was helping a niggah eat and get his energy up. Fuck nah, I'm not letting a niggah jack shit! Homies were trying to take food out of my mouth and fuck up my friendship. They weren't looking at that part though. Top it off, my guy was only charging me thirty-eight hunnid for nine of them and wasn't charging shit but three twenty-five for the trees. They weren't feeling I wouldn't let them jack him though. They weren't feeling my situation. They weren't giving a damn about my belly being full, they were just on me tripping and not letting them get at my guy. Fuck what I was going through, fuck me eating, it was about them and me not letting them eat.

"Fuck that donkey cuz, we're the homies!"..."You're going against the homies for a punk ass donkey!" Yeah, pretty much, it wasn't going to happen. I'm already knowing too it was the homie on some funny shit! "Fuck cuz too!"..."That ain't the homie, the homie would let a niggah eat

## FEELING SOME TYPE OF WAY—SODO AUSTIN

too!" This, that and the third. Yeah, I know I probably was all types of bitch ass niggahs! "Punk ass niggahs!" But like I told them too, "Do you really think he came by himself, just b'cuz you don't see anyone but him?" The illusion of truth again wearing a mask of deception well. I told them that though, just in case they decided to shoot their shot anyway. Not the illusion part I just spoke on but the "Do you really think he came by himself?" part. I wanted to put that on their minds.

    Some dudes don't use common sense and have tunnel vision when they're keyed in on shit. It's all about what they on, that's it, that's all! These days common sense ain't so common. One particular time, my connect came through and dropped off the work. I had a homie at the spot with me, one of the homies who had wanted to jack him. After me and my guy finished conducting our "B.I." (business), I walked him back outside and stood on the porch watching him. I watched him get in his "swoop" then pull off after a couple of minutes. After he pulled off, like always, another swoop pulled out right behind him before he cleared the block. I just shook my head, thinking about my Mickey ass homies. Did they really think he wouldn't have nobody else with him? (SMH) Apparently so, huh? All he does is ride around all day, drop off work and pick up rabbs. Dudes have to be on dope, dick and dynamite! He's never slipping like that. They know about thirsty mutha fuckas.

    The few times the homies saw him, they just happened to be in the spot, never saw him coming, never watched him leave. So to my knowledge, they were clueless as to the 2nd swoop that followed him closely. Most definitely it wasn't going to be a good look, it was no bueno!

## FEELING SOME TYPE OF WAY—SODO AUSTIN

They're cautious as a mutha fucka, they're never sleep at the wheel. It's not amateur hour! If anybody know niggahs, it's Paisas who know niggahs! But yeah, the homies were feeling some type of way about that for a hot ass minute, b'cuz they felt I went against them for a Mexican. I mean, shit, I couldn't help how they felt. They weren't worried about how I felt or I couldn't help how they thought. They were going to have whatever thoughts they were going to have. Bottom line, I wasn't fucking with them on that.

It wasn't going down like that, period, point blank! I was on my rabb shit, trying to eat, just like my connect was. Fuck that, he was straight with me and letting me win, so I was going to keep it straight with him, all one hunnid. I wasn't about to let a niggah do shit. Yeah, I had a few instances where I wasn't a fan of the homies. Some I really didnt give a fuck about being a fan of anyway and it was whatever, they weren't gang bang anyway! Like an instance I had spoke on the BG and G homies, when we had had that secret meeting in the G homie's Dirty Reds Shop on a late night hype and the BG's were told not to bring no "bangers" (guns).

That was one of those go against the grain type instances b'cuz niggahs had life and bullshit fucked up, suuuper! These are gang gang G homies that's with the bullshit and they all play ball! So, based on, BG's would've been horseplaying not to put some type of security into play, in case some shit would've gotten out of hand. Anything less would be a misoverstanding in our eyes, I wasn't feeling that. I was one of the first BG's to be on some, "That's just not a good look, walking in a situation that could potentially go sideways off the dribble. Go sideways quick, fast and in a hurry, b'cuz these are G homies that can go from zero to sixty on some shit, and it was a heated type situation.

Somebody could've said something that had the G homies working with F and E's, feeling some type of way and it would've went up (got active) off the dribble. I wasn't going to be comfortable being in a situation, a heated one at that, "not be heated" and was told not to have no bangers too. Nah...that was out! My antennas went up immediately. There's nothing like a lil security on the situation, it wasn't just going to be a BG getting the bad end of that "B.I." A few of us stepped in heated too, I can bang that! Three of them for sure. Them being not heated highly unlikely. They're never horseplaying. That's because I know their get down and history, they're really gang gang. Now the G homie Dirty Red who's shop it was and who was playing intermediator told us not to bring no banger, I couldn't say for sure or not. If he did though trust...the G homies were thinking like some of us were and went against the grain too, knowing their young homies.

Just like them, we had reputables too that was gang gang and with the bullshit, known to put in work...active! Gang gang recognotice gang gang and respect other gang gangs, young or old, that's just the reality of it. On the side of caution, that's what niggahs was going to do, go against the grain. Have to respect it, though for what and as it was. On some other shit, I would never discourage a niggah to not go against the grain. For what? Do what you do. If that's your position as a man, who am I to knock your get down? Handle your wax and sag it out. Going against the grain is the easiest shit b'cuz that's just my personality and my nature to say fuck

## FEELING SOME TYPE OF WAY—SODO AUSTIN

it! If I see something that isn't a good look, or I'm not feeling it, I'm against it.

I'm not going to be complicit nor condone any Gilliganism, or go along with it, in any type of way. It's no bueno! I don't do the pressure up thing when I'm forced to choose sides. I don't engage, especially when it comes to homies or internal shit in the turf. I don't get involved and I'm remaining neutral. That's me going against the grain. Homies wanted to jack I.C. at the time that I fucked with him on a daily. It got back to me, you already know, no bueno! But as soon as I got "wrapped up" and out of the turf, it didn't take long after that before homies got him. It was a matter of time before it was going to happen though. He was a Gilligan with bitch niggah ways. That's why we ended up falling out and cutting ties. When I heard it, while I'm at Solano, that the homies jacked him and ran him out of the turf, it didn't surprise me. It was something they'd been wanting to do. It was just easier doing it with me out of the "captured moment." I thought I would've been got that memo. Cold thing about it, he don't even live in the City no more. He basically got out of dodge and went up north (Northern California). That didn't surprise me either, him getting jacked by the homies and him bouncing up and out of the City. I ain't going to lie. I found the whole situation amusing. I laughed my ass off, just based on. I will be the first to admit, though, going against the grain can have major consequences, could have. An all praise is due to Allah, to Allah we belong and to Him we return moment, could end your career.

It definitely fuck off relationships, bonds and ties. Definitely will have niggahs working with F and E's, feeling some type of way, you're

## FEELING SOME TYPE OF WAY—SODO AUSTIN

going to be the bad guy. Fucking with the homies, they aren't going to be feeling you or the situation, depending what it is and what your status is. You might find yourself a victim of the homies, I can bang that! Do be mindful of that look, it don't come without cost, especially if you're not a reputable homie and homies aren't feeling you, wasn't feeling you, prior to you going against the grain.

    Homies will be on some fuck that niggah or whatever it was that got dudes riled up and fuck you too, you're not just the bad guy, you're the bagged guy. I mean, even with me, I still kept my eyes on certain dudes and stayed checking for temperatures, even though it appeared to be nothing once dudes appeared to have gotten over the bullshit. Until I felt comfortable with it, I stayed checking, never fully letting my guard down. Until then, it was a hot ass seventeen rounds in the clip, one in the "brain" (chamber) and I'm off safety, ready to go. Then there's the flip side of it, where a homie's going against the grain on something that you're pushing for and got you feeling some type of way and working with F and E's. I had got into it with this niggah that stayed in some apartments where homies stayed (Big Half Pint and Tumac) on the North Side of the "Beach" (Long Beach). The homie Tumac knew me and this dude got into it and had words. It was going to be an issue if I caught this dude in traffic. I just happen to be pushing up the block (Linden) on foot and who do I see coming out of ole boy's spot (dude), the one I had words with and the homie Tumac. I'm like wow...for real! I'm not going to lie, I was in my feelings. I made sure the homie saw me see him coming out of dude's spot with him (SMH). I point at him. Yeah, I see you, and I was nodding my

## FEELING SOME TYPE OF WAY—SODO AUSTIN

head up and down...down and up, on some, "Yeah, I see you!" Known for being gang gang and with the pistol play, I assume he was spooked...suuuper! I felt he was going against the grain for a bitch ass niggah, not even from the turf. A'ight, I get he's your neighbor and you fucked with the niggah, but to me and me being high, it looked like some other shit was at play.

That's how it looked to me and how I took it. Apparently, he took it the same way, as far as thinking what he thought I was thinking and went somewhere else with it. I was thinking something foul was going on, like he was plotting on me with dude. So him feeling however he was feeling, called the next niggah on me. The very same dude I was speaking on in "Yard Life" (Exposé, Real Life Inside Of Prison) that had an issue with me and my religion. Anyway, he calls him to intervene, if in fact it was a situation to be calmed or intervened (SMH). Yeah, that boomerang gang is a mutha fucka. It's a fucked up feeling when the rabbit has the banger. Yeah, got you feeling some type of way and working with F and E's. Feeling like a niggah going against you, what you stand on and what you're about.

Fuck you and fuck how you feel. Have you like, "Fuck the world! Fuck this niggah! Fuck them niggahs!" I've been on both ends of that spectrum, so I overstand it and all the elements that make it up. A couple of times when the Chuck Taylor was on the other foot, I was feeling some type of way to the point I wanted to bag a mutha fucka! Bag 'em on some arrogant shit, like who's this dude to go against me for this, that or the

## FEELING SOME TYPE OF WAY—SODO AUSTIN

third reason? I can see how the next dude can feel how he feel and be working with the feelings he's working with. Mind you, I was out there off of that water too, for those that didn't know. I was on some bullshit, at times. This dude's against you, these dudes against you. See how quick a dude was willing to go against you at the slightest provocation?

See how quick they tried to dismiss what you were saying? I do overstand don't nobody like feeling like a mutha fucka's going against them. They're going to be working with F and E's and feeling some type of way, I can bang that too! So when you're going against the grain, be mindful of what could come of it and what is or who it is you're taking a stand against. On this note though, if it's a situation involving snitching, I can overstand a niggah going against the grain. A niggah should always go against the grain in that sense. Fuck a snitch! Fuck everything he's about and represent. Dude's a scumbag and don't deserve to be breathing. That's just keeping it a hunnid, strictly my belief and view on it. If it was up to me, I'll put their ass on a deserted island with a bunch of wild ass animals and no means to defend or protect themselves. Just snitches against wild ass animals in their natural habitat.

Any dude feeling some type of way b'cuz you're not down with protecting a snitch or allowing yourself to be bought by one, allowing them to pay their way out of being fucked over for horseplaying, fuck them too, straight up. As far as I'm concerned, if they're getting down like that (condoning snitching or protecting a snitch), they're suspect. Why wouldn't they be? Being a part of anything that has to do with snitches or their activity? Me, I'm straight, I'm not fucking with it unless it's removing

## FEELING SOME TYPE OF WAY—SODO AUSTIN

their snitching ass...rat bastard! As my saying goes, "A snitch anywhere is a threat to real niggahs everywhere!" I stand by that, I live by that and fuck who don't share that sentiment in regards to that...fuck you! Mean that in every sense of the words...fuck you! And the air you breathe! The very air you breathe.

How are you going to protect, hide or fuck with a snitch? B'cuz here it is, you call yourself a "street niggah," a "real niggah" or gang gang! Not a damn thing "street...real...or...gang gang about a niggah like that and I can bang that, on the turf! Show me street...show me real...show me gang gang, make or convince me that that's street, real or gang gang. You can shoot your shot, but nah, it's not going to happen.

Then has the nerve to be in your feelings b'cuz the next dude isn't feeling it or fucking with it...straight horseplaying! Know why you're not feeling it or fucking with it? Riddle me that. Want me to tell you? It's b'cuz they know that shit's foul, foul as fuck. I'm going to go against the grain every fucking time, I'm never not going against the grain. A niggah can't ever convince me to support him on anything that has anything to do with a snitch niggah! Unless we're bagging him, not in this lifetime or the next one. I fucking hate snitches with a passion. Can't convince me of nothing in regards to the shenanigans of a snitch or the support of one...no bueno! I can't do it, won't do it and refuse to do it. That's the ultimate sin to me. Being a snitch, condoning a snitch or harboring him.

Don't even get at me about no shit like that, don't even think we're that cool to get at me on no shit like that. Your feelings will be hurt along

## FEELING SOME TYPE OF WAY—SODO AUSTIN

with your ego and possibly your mutha fuckin jaw! We're never, ever that cool, just so you know, that's a no go for Sodo! Don't get it, me or life confused! I'm not "him" homie, ain't ever going to be him. I rather meet Allah before I'm that guy! Miss me entirely with those funnies or shenanigans! With that shit period. "See no evil...hear no evil...speak no evil!" I'm going to always go against the grain when it has anything to do with that type of shit and will go against a mutha fucka that don't go against that grain. I'm not fucking with you and better hope a niggah don't catch you on a late night hype in the turf, just hanging out all willy nilly like it's all gravity! And I ain't seen.

Yeah, you might fuck around and have an issue on your hand. One of them, all praise is due Allah, to Allah we belong and to Him we return kind of issue, making it make sense. Since a mutha fucka pulled his batteries out (gave up, tapped out, etc.), why not keep them out? Yeah, that's how I go against the grain, on some real shit, suuuper! I'll go against the grain when it has anything to do with that type of shit. I don't protect snitches, don't fuck with them or don't harbor them, none of that weirdo shit! I don't help to harbor them, none of that weird shit either, get a bar (pay attention). I'm strictly anti-snitch and anti-niggah who fuck with them on any capacity, family by blood included, I don't discriminate.

The only ones I don't trip off of are the citizens, that's expected of them (don't condone or support their shit, either), they're not in the life or live by the code of the streets. They're not of the streets or in the streets though it's foul and frowned upon behavior. As a street dude in the field, I can't hold them to that standard of living. They're not in the streets committing crime and breaking the law. They're playing by the rules and a part of it for them is reporting shit they see or know (SMH). Still a rat bastard though, in the opinion of the streets. I don't worry myself with citizens, I just stay out of their way doing and being me, trying my damnest not to let them see or know shit. B'cuz if they get on me and put me out there, then that was my bad for allowing myself to slip and to the point I was reckless and not paying attention. Can't be mad at them or feeling some type of way with them for doing what you expected them to do from jump.

    Yeah, it's contradictory to my belief, but that's just reality as it is, for what it is. But yeah, don't fix your mouth to ask me about anything in relation to fucking with a snitch or harboring them. I'm telling you off the top...no bueno! You're going to meet resistance, some harsh words and probably flighted. You know who's with that shit, keep the line moving and go where they're doing it at. Yeah, so my so-called big homie, who I no longer fuck with, don't think I found out about him harboring one, after I got wrapped up and was no longer on the streets. To my overstanding, only a handful actually knew the "B.I." To be honest, it didn't surprise me, not in the least bit. He knew where a dude was the whole time this niggah was being looked for by the homies. Not only did he know, he was talking to him on a daily and when the niggah would sneak back in the City to his people's (family) spot on the North, he would fuck with him and hang out with him like it was cool and shit. (Alright.) (SMH)

    I was like wow initially. At the end of the day though, I suspected it, just wasn't sure, but then it came to light years later, as all things do

## FEELING SOME TYPE OF WAY—SODO AUSTIN

that's in the dark. Shit in the dark and it's foul is going to always reveal itself, it's just the way of the world, it's funny that way. He knew niggahs were looking for that dude, even hung out, late ,"in the cut" (concealed), around his area hoping to catch him coming or going, but never did or could. When it's all said and done, he wasn't a banger, he rode skateboards initially. He just fell into character, making himself fit the equation. It wasn't him...period, point blank. Hanging out with him, even I hung out with him and blew blunts with him. I fucked with him, but being older, I had sense not to do shit around him or talk around him. I kept my dealings with him limited. He was cool and all of that, but shit, it was clearly seen he wasn't built for the lifestyle in general or the shit that came with it. Cold thing about it, niggahs were telling the lil homies that fucked with him, "Y'all shouldn't be fucking with cuz on the tip y'all are fucking with him on!" ..."Y'all need to stop having him around so much and having him around when certain shit's going on or taking place."

"Stop taking turf B.I. around cuz, especially shit he wasn't around for or didn't see or know about. He's going to be the reason, watch and see, mark my words." Did they listen? Nah! Fuck Nah, their young ass didn't listen. "Cuz straight!" "We know him, he's solid as fuck!" He saw and knew too much, way more than he should've been allowed to. He knew way too much and for his own good, if you ask me personally. I'm surprised he didn't tell a lot sooner than he did. He tried holding out, I guess, but when they started talking about life, this, that and the third, and he was pressured up, fuck a canary, that niggah got to singing like Luther! (SMH) "I...know...who...shot...that...dude...and...where...he...live...whoo

## FEELING SOME TYPE OF WAY—SODO AUSTIN

whoo whoo." I can just see his soft ass sitting up in there spilling the beans. (SMH) Doing what bitch niggahs do!

Fuck nah, they didn't listen, going against the grain and it's a dude with all day (life) behind that niggah getting his Luther on. But what's so crazy, the same dude he told on is accused of the same thing. (SMH) Accused of speaking on my "boy...boy!" Oh yeah, they tried to their damnest to wash my boy up, he didn't allow them to. He shot his shot and jumped off the train! Anything less, my niggah was dunzo! He knew not to keep going against the grain playing with them b'cuz at some point they were going to be on some, "Ain't no deal, let's run this shit and it might not of been a good look for the homie. He's good though, some instances it don't be a good look going against the grain, especially if it's your life or freedom on the line. Live or stay free to fight another day. That's to all my street niggahs, my real niggahs, homies or not and most definitely to my Bitterchild nation!

FEELING SOME TYPE OF WAY—SODO AUSTIN

## "In The City Niggah"

Like them shots going off in the City niggah
Boy what it cost, niggahs play for keeps and ah
Put you at ah loss, sanity decrease, it's ah
Lesson to be taught...

Is there ah lesser of the two evils, foul come from
Gene pools, niggahs calling audibles, fucking up the rules
Homie, real niggah optional...

I put my hand on the Bible, will they ever cop to it?
Snitches turn rivals, ah situation had you blow it, niggahs
Lay idled, signs getting ran through...

In ah land of survival, bitch niggahs confrontational
You can quote me, niggah shoot those, heavily devoted,
Real niggahs expose niggahs...

Got 'em coming up short, pressure ah have 'em folding, ah
Niggah destiny been wrote, ah get it cracking from the
Shoulders, gottah keep focus...

Too easy to turn ghost, eyes gon get closed, like
Time never frozen, wicketry send 'em floating, trees and

## FEELING SOME TYPE OF WAY—SODO AUSTIN

Water got it heightened...

Niggahs moving bogus, wonder why we fight 'em,
Seeing the turf through ah scope, homies stay colliding,
Beefing ain't ah joke, no joke...

Niggahs ah get it wilding, politicians got us voting,
Ah niggah off the island, shock and with no hope, ah
Niggah got his ride on...

Making it hard to cope, while we getting blowed
Though, sag it out to the fullest, Killing off them
Notions, when niggahs on they bullshit...

Like them shots going off in the City niggah
Boy what it cost, niggahs play for keeps and ah
Put you at ah loss, sanity decrease, it's ah
Lesson to be taught...

# Chapter 7

## "What You Signed Up For"

What you signed up for is basically you obligating yourself to any and every aspect of the politics of a dude being a banger or a dude being a street niggah. You signed up for everything anticipated and for the shit you didn't anticipate basically. Shit...feeling some type of way and working with feelings and emotions (F and E's) are just a part of it, as with being "wrapped up" (going to jail) or having an all praise is due Allah, to Allah we belong and to Him we return moment, as with you having to put yours on the line for a Gilligan ass niggah who wouldn't put his on the line for you (SMH), not by a long shot! He's sticking to the self preservation script. It fucks with your mental when you find out shit wasn't what you thought it was, it's no doubt a reality check. Homies not having love for homies like they say they do, it's only an interest until it isn't. Once the interest shit is moved the homie shit is too. Homies aren't what they once were when they really were gang gang! There's a lot of separatism, shenanigans and dirty politics.

Homies aren't fucking with homies, homies aren't respecting the game for what and as it really is, it's being played with and disrespected by Mickey homies, by fake dudes, playing a part that they're really not with or about. All the backbiting that goes on, all the shady politics that goes viral, all the homie on homie Mickey shit, all the snitching that goes on and the complicity in it (SMH). I sit back a lot of times reflecting and be like dayum! This is the shit a niggah's a part of and have signed up for

## FEELING SOME TYPE OF WAY—SODO AUSTIN

(SMH). This shit is foul as fuck! And most definitely watered down, especially nowadays you can't trust mutha fuckas! It wouldn't be a wise decision with all the fuckery and shenanigans in play. You can't be all willy-nilly with trusting dudes claiming homie, every dude claiming homie ain't homie! Especially a niggah saying, "You can trust me!" Me personally, I don't up and trust a mutha fucka, that's all the way out! That's no bueno!

I'm not trusting a mutha fucka as far as I can throw their mutha fuckin ass! You really don't know who to trust with all this bullshit going on and the games that are being played. You don't know who's loyal to who, who really fucks with who. You can't just assume shit to be as it appears. Illusions are a constant presence, as with homies playing ball on homies and bagging them...no surprise though...whaaat! It's even harder trying to separate the real shit from the fake shit, the real niggahs from the fake niggahs! They look so much alike (SMH). Just when you thought you got it figured out, up pops the weasel, here comes another look of it, in a different shape or form, from a different angle in the field of play. All the bullshit constantly changes, it's the same shit just a different look. Just when you thought you've seen it all, you come to recognotice you haven't and can never see it all, it's always going to be something else. Something different that's going to come along and piss on you. You'll come to learn, know and overstand the illusions of truths wearing that mask of deception and wearing it well.

## FEELING SOME TYPE OF WAY—SODO AUSTIN

You'll come to learn, know and overstand imminent death and jail knocking at dude's doors, knock often as fuck too! You'll come to learn, know and overstand all praise is due to Allah, to Allah we belong and to Him we return moments. You'll come to learn, know and overstand fear, pain, regret, choices, consequences, life, jealousy, hatred and loss. As you'll come to learn, know and overstand when to humble yourself and when to shoot your shot on pressing play, or when to not overstep boundaries or cross certain lines. Without a doubt though you'll find your perception altered with a whole lot of shit, due in part to a dude's elements and surroundings, questioning shit. Yeah, you'll come to do that, questioning niggah's motives or agendas, as with their moral compass and integrity. I can bang that too! Shit just isn't going to add up in certain instances with certain dudes or with certain situations or make sense to you sometimes. That's just what it is.

It's a'ight though, you're supposed to question shit when you're not feeling it, especially when it's not making sense or adding up, shit does be suspect. Dudes damn sure be, get a bar, Autobot! Dudes' movements are suspect, conversations and actions, all of that shit be suspect. All you have to do though, is pay attention, they stay exposing themselves. Time reveals. Dudes tend to use a lot of trickery and wordplay, they're good at what they do, as far as "Autobotism" and dirty ball playing, with their instances where its cool to do certain shit or certain shit doesn't apply for some but others. Basically on some whatever fits the equation or narrative at the moment type shit. Yet they expect dudes not to feel some type of way. Dudes be having life and bullshit fucked up, suuuper! But shit, can't fault them for trying to shoot their shot, it's what dudes do. Checking aint cheating, huh? That's what they say...yeah, what the fuck ever, a niggah's testing his hand. Slow your roll Turbo! Yeah, slow your roll Turbo! Once you start seeing certain shit, seeing niggahs do certain shit, questionable shit, you start to analyze shit and seeing shit and dudes for what they really are and as they really are.

As it really is though, not that "cut" (diluted) shit, just reality, you're not going to feel homies or feel the same way about what it is you're representing. Seeing how it's being played with, seeing how dudes aren't loyal to it, not respecting it, or respecting the fact dudes are being bagged for this shit (representing the turf and being gang gang) and bagged behind it. To see the shit that's being seen, it's like dudes are dying in vain, dudes got banged (shot) in vain, being bussed on in vain. The shit dudes are being allowed to get away with on the streets and in the maze (prison), the stunts pulled and not being held accountable for their actions, it's just crazy (SMH). Dudes do the most, homies allowing homies to snitch and still be in the turf, knowing niggahs are snitching (SMH). Where do they do that at? Everywhere, that's where! In your turf, my turf and in the next dude's turf. Dudes should know when they snitch, their career as they knew it to be is O.V.E.R.!...Eastside!

Dun mutha fuckin zo (dunzo). They should always feel pressured up and shouldn't ever feel like they can snitch and have a way out! Feeling like dudes are going to harbor them or feel like if they have rabbs they can hit a few dudes that they feel count or are gang gang and get a pass...uh, no bueno! They should always feel like their ass is on a turn (trouble),

## FEELING SOME TYPE OF WAY—SODO AUSTIN

supposed to stay looking over their shoulders...whaaat! But there it is. You have dudes changing the play and the rules, making this shit up as they go, as Gilligans do, as Autobots do, as dirty ball players do! Have dudes picking and choosing what's acceptable and what isn't, choosing what shit should be tripped off of and what shit shouldn't be (SMH). Picking and choosing shouldn't be no where in the equation when it's foul. K.T.S.E.! How can you pick and choose what telling count as telling and what telling don't count as telling? When it's telling, it's telling, period.

    A ball is a ball and a strike is a strike. Me personally, I was under the impression all telling was telling, period, point blank, there's no grey area, it is what it is. "He only said a lil bit, oh he only said this, that and the third." That was just a report, that wasn't a transcript. What is a statement being made? Riddle me that. What is the difference between a transcript and a report? Riddle me that. Me playing Bitterchild advocate again, not a damn thing. Ain't a difference and I'll bet a thousand more mutha fuckas will stress the same. It's something dudes say on record and its printed in black and white (paperwork). "The Ones" (police) didn't just pull that shit out of their ass, damn sure didn't pull it out of thin air, it come from somewhere. The somewhere came from a mutha fuckas mouth making a statement. Then you have justification for fucking with these foul ass dudes, and with a mindset of "Shit, he aint tell on me, I ain't tripping!" (SMH) So basically you acknowledge a niggah telling, but since he didnt tell on you, it's all gravity! Wow! These are the type of dudes youre dealing with an are surrounded by on a daily, dudes with these type of mindsets.

## FEELING SOME TYPE OF WAY—SODO AUSTIN

Dudes with the audacity to harbor these snitching ass niggahs and accept shit from them, giving them a pass, ain't that a bitch! But they want to lead you to believe they're the real dudes! There's nothing real about a dude harboring or protecting a snitch or giving his snitch ass a pass. What's real about you? You hear all the time how dudes had gotten wrapped up and their homies are allowing dudes to still come around and be in the turf. I know there's a "gang" (a lot) of dudes from everywhere that's feeling some type of way about their homies. "Fuck them niggahs...fuck that niggah!" "Got such and such snitch ass in the turf and ain't nobody done shit to him." "I called over such and such spot and such and such over there posted up." (SMH) I shake my head every time I hear it. It's like you expect something different, but the results are same...really? Some dudes do play fair though, some do respect it for what and as it is...uh-huh.

Still pushing by that code and pushing them same ole school "G" niggahs ethics, real niggah values, real niggahs morals, remaining unswayed and unmoved by the bullshit dudes push and how they're pushing it. Stay calling dudes out on their bullshit, but these are the homies and dudes that find themselves politicked on and found slumped and bagged some mutha fuckin where, easy call! (SMH) A case of nobody knows who done it. Trust and believe though, someone knows something. Dudes are going to stay feeling some type of way about a dude going against their equation, any dude with a name or without one, or one that's going to put up with any type of resistance in supporting a push they're for,

## FEELING SOME TYPE OF WAY—SODO AUSTIN

with or about. Going to push to turn dudes against you and have them looking at you sideways and feeling some type of way.

Based on them not feeling being called on their bullshit. Like, why are you doing it (calling them on it) and other homies aren't? Not feeling a dude always having shit to say about something they have going on. Yeah, let that be the reason. Reasons will stay being looked for to politic a dude and to have that narrative justified in their mind and in the Autobot's mind. Then comes the bullshit being in play. Dudes and their bullshit! Depending what it is and how it's presented, a situation can get real Mickey and potentially separate the turf, causing internal beef and homies choosing sides. Choosing the wrong side though, can be Mickey too and can go all bad, suuuper! Internal beefs have homies pressured up! They're no jokes, based on dudes knowing where dudes lay their heads at, where they be at and where dudes post up. It's easy to play ball. Sometimes it's just homies lining up, with homies on sight, or homies are catching other homies slipping in traffic and "pack them out" (jump them).

Do it go to "ball playing" (shooting)? It can and it does, and it has went to homies "bussing on homies" (shooting homies), bussing at homies, the whole nine yards. Sad to say, but that's just what it is, that's just reality and fact of the matter. Homies buss on and at homies, just like they bag them. Shit, some turfs probably have more bags by on their own hands than enemigo do or just as many, and I can bang that! This is the shit dudes sign up for when they were "put on" (initiated). You signed up to be told on, you signed up to be faked on, you signed up to be hated on and left for dead. You signed up to be turned on and have homies backbite you. You signed up to be pressured up, for a homie to run out on you and not keep it a hunnid. You signed up for a homie to jack you or set you up, given the chance and could be gotten away with.

You signed up to be DP'ed, disappointed and let down, by homies you thought were homies. This is the shit you signed up for? Absolutely not! Nah, you're not going to be told this is what you're signing up for when you got put on. That's just shit you're going to come to learn, know and overstand with time, seeing the shit you see. Given you hadn't gotten spooked and tapped out or pulled your batteries out. A lot of times, we've signed up for shit that we realize we got in over our heads, being it's under false pretenses or not. It's a cold thing when you come to realize shit wasn't what you thought or what it seemed. Come to realize dudes weren't who you thought they were. A realization that will actually have you like, "Damn, so that is what it is all along," and is going to have you feeling some type of way. A lot of shit you come to learn, you're not going to feel or agree with, and it's going to have you feeling some type of way about it, working with F and E's! You'll come to learn your overstanding isn't the same as other homies and certain homies when it comes to representing the turf and representing it as it's supposed to be represented. You'll see how banging (gang banging) isn't for everyone, as you see, every niggah that says he's a homie isn't a homie. You can't help but to come to that realization. Dudes become transparent and they expose themselves after a while, the gig is up! Just b'cuz a dude says he's a homie don't make him a homie...fact! Just b'cuz you represent the same turf don't make a niggah a homie. I've learned that one years ago.

## FEELING SOME TYPE OF WAY—SODO AUSTIN

Dude's mouth says one thing but their actions say something else entirely. "BND" (bullshit niggah detector) is going off. (SMH) A dude doesn't have to say he's a homie if he's actually a real homie. His actions are going to reflect that and what his homie'ism is about and whether or not he's gang gang, point blank, period...real shit! To be perfectly honest with you, "homie" is so overrated, especially these days, no substance. It's just a word that these dudes throw around loosely as a part of the shared common interest. In the "maze" or on the streets. Just like niggahs and bitches throw "love" around loosely, no substance behind it or in it, it's just a word, being on their dick and pussy shit! (A situationship). Just thrown around like it isn't shit, have no meaning or value. It's the same shit with niggahs and the word homie. "That's the homie...he the homie...homie this, homie that, homie the third...sup, homie?" What makes me the homie b'cuz I say it to you? Riddle me that. What makes you the homie b'cuz you said I was the homie?

Personally, I'd rather a dude just say he fucks with me and we're straight than for him to call me homie or say we're homies when we aren't homies. I can be a homie, but overstand my homie'ism isn't the next dude's homie'ism or my definition of homie isn't the next dude's definition of homie. I'm quick to tell a dude, though, off the dribble, just b'cuz a dude will say he's a homie doesn't mean he's one. I'm quick to call a ball a ball and a strike a strike. A dude will say some shit b'cuz. You have to be mindful of dudes just using the word homie for the homie card.

Homie this! Homie that! Homie the third! Homie the other! When they're trying to get you to assist them or trying to get something up out of

## FEELING SOME TYPE OF WAY—SODO AUSTIN

you, "Yeah, you're the homie like a mutha fucka!" What you come to overstand when you're keeping it "too too" real too, dudes will go out of their way to assassinate your character and try to downplay your activiteness or your get down. They'll even find some type of way to politic on you, that's just what dudes do. Oh, don't let a dude not like you or feel you or just feeling some type of way about you. He's on some hoe shit with his Autobots...suuuper! Will look for a reason, some instances dudes will go way back when on some old shit to trip off of. He done such and such anyway back then. (SMH) Straight Mickey shit!

That's just to justify why whatever happened to you happened to you. (SMH) That's the same way dudes do dudes that snitched too. A dude could've snitched and nothing was ever done. Years and years could've went by but then he does something not felt, blooom! Niggah's bagged like a mutha fucka...up and out of here, see you! Then its... "Fuck that niggah, he was snitching anyway!" Whaaat! Like that wasn't already viral. (SMH) Dudes are something else (SMH). With games and how they play them, the shit is crafty as fuck. Dudes knew for years and years he was a rat bastard and had snitched, but all of a sudden niggahs are feeling some type of way. If you don't knock it the fuck off! Then here comes the justification. He was a snitch anyway. That's been overstood...shit that was justifiable years and years ago, weird ass niggahs! Dudes will just speak on a dude being a snitch but won't do shit until it's something they're tripping off of personally.

Only b'cuz they're feeling a certain type of way, it's an issue. You should've been feeling some type of way and in your feels. Cuz been a snitch, he should've been voted off the island. Oh, but since you're tripping off of him it's an issue, now he has to walk the plank! He gotta go, plans already in motion to get rid of dude...play, he has been pressed! (SMH) That's how dudes operate though, and how they get down. They won't and don't trip off certain shit or certain dudes until it's something they're tripping off of and in their feels about. Before then it's gravity. It's always some pick a choose type shit with dudes, K.T.S.E.! (SMH) It's a separation of blocks dudes are all from the same turf, dudes do hang with certain dudes on different blocks though. You know it's always a social ladder. There's always homies that are gang gang with a bigger presence, the "in crowd." The in crowd dudes hang over here with these dudes. The dudes that aren't a part of that crowd hang over there. There's always two parties, like Democrats and Republicans, the "in crowd" and the "out crowd." It's always been that way. Gang gang dudes fuck with gang gang dudes on a constant basis, these are the in crowd. Every block of the turf has their dudes that stand out from the crowd.

However, certain dudes and certain blocks you aren't trying to fuck with you like that if you're not gang gang, that's just a proven fact, it's a social status too. You'll never really see a lamb type dude hanging with hyenas (SMH). You have crews and cliques, period, point blank, that messes with each other. You even have crews and cliques beefing with each other, that's a given. You have dudes that look down on dudes that be on and hang on certain blocks, just as you have dudes being looked at funny and looked at sideways. Sideways for fucking with certain dudes or for hanging with certain dudes. Some reasons could be valid and legit, but

## FEELING SOME TYPE OF WAY—SODO AUSTIN

some could be Autobot driven or b'cuz dudes are "emo niggahs" and working with feelings (SMH).

Sometimes it doesn't have to be a reason at all, period, dudes are feeling some type of way. Homies are just known for tripping on homies, backbiting homies, plotting on homies, politicing on homies, jacking homies, switching up on homies, banging (shooting) homies, bagging homies, the whole nine yards. It's a dirty game period, even more so now in these 2000's. It's flat out common practice, especially the telling on homies (SMH), common occurrences, a ball is a ball and a strike is a strike! Get a bar, the shit's Mickey! It is what it is at the end of the day. But yeah, dudes need to know, overstand and feel what it is they're signing up for. This shit is real, very real, and isn't a joke or game by no means. It's raw, it's uncut, it's real in the field. Gets realer and can get even realer. From the outside looking in, it's a mirage, an illusion.

Trust me when I say it, it's never what you it appears to be, not by a long shot. Like I've stressed, gang banging or being a gang member isn't for everybody. Everybody isn't cut out for the lifestyle. It's just a lot going on. Like the streets aren't for everybody, it's really a lot going on there. Everybody isn't made or built for this shit. That's part of the reason shit's fucked up, dudes are coming up off of the porch before they're ready to, trying to jump in feet first. (SMH) Jumping in, thinking it's a game and when they see it isn't, they're caught up. They either get on some bullshit and be on some bullshit, b'cuz they fell in with the wrong crowd or something ends up happening and they're pressured up, and now they're telling! Telling some mo shit!

## FEELING SOME TYPE OF WAY—SODO AUSTIN

What I know and overstand today in "2022" I wouldn't advise or suggest dudes to engage in gang banging or whatever you want to call it, it's played out, watered down and simply bullshit. That's just keeping it a hunnid! Straight up! This shit is foul and suuuper watered down, like drink...in a club. Dudes aren't shit, banging ain't shit, there's no loyalty, no trust, no real homies, no real turf'ism, no real camaraderie, just common and self interest, with a whole lot of dirty ball being played. That's my assessment, but to each is own. The shit that's going on today, dudes shouldn't want to be a part of...really, flag on the play! Death or jail is coming even faster than anticipated, based on the elements, by large, of today's gang banging and how dudes are moving and quick to press play on shit.

    Don't get me wrong, it's been fucked up, it's just more fucked up even more so now, adding the gang drugs into the mix, your heroin, crystal, your pills, weed and sherm has always been there. Oh, can't forget the "powder" (SMH). Most of the shit that's going on now is gang drug driven. That just put a whole different spin on it, bringing a whole different element to the already fucked up situation. Young homie, from me to you, it ain't cool! It's clearly seen and so transparent how dudes are getting down with each other and on each other. A cold piece of B.I. and hearing all of the stories of how dudes are getting down. that's me suuuper talking to you late ass bloomers trying to jump in the lane, eighteen, nineteen, twenty, want to start gang banging. Dude, if you don't knock it the hell off! And go sit your ass down somewhere! Sit...down! Really, sit down somewhere! (SMH) If you weren't doing it before then (gang banging) why bother? You might as well leave it the fuck alone. Go on and do something else with yourself. It's not for you, leave the bullshit where the bullshit at, it's not really what you're looking for, trust me! It's not what you want, my dude. Again, I wouldn't recommend it or advise it. If I had to do it all over again, I wouldn't fuck with it, I would be straight as Indian hair on it, and that's straight! Knowing what I know now, it would've been no bueno! Seeing what I see and have seen, that's out! (SMH) Want no part of it, that's just keeping it a hunnid...I'm cool! Though I knew what I signed up for (gang banging), I didn't sign up for all of the other shit that came along with it. That part!

    The foul shit, the dirty politics, the snitching, the hater'ism, or the homie on homie shit didn't sign up for that look. That shit right there is on a whole different level of gang banging and politics (SMH). Don't get me wrong though, if I had to bang or bag a niggah that's supposed to be a homie and it's justified and not on no dirty shit or jealous shit, his ass is going to get hollered at, banged or bagged. It's as simple as that. Like I was saying at the beginning of this chapter, where I saying you're having to put yours on the line (freedom or life) for a dude you know isn't going to reciprocate that same energy. Especially when you're in the maze on a yard. You can already see what a dude's on. He's half ass and he's suspect, but you can't actually know or see for sure what's what until you're up against the wall.

    Up against the wall and going through it, or a situation comes about exposing the real for what it really is. But quick to say that he's with it or about it, this, that and the third. When it's all said and done though,

## FEELING SOME TYPE OF WAY—SODO AUSTIN

You'll find yourself disappointed, telling yourself I should've known this niggah was a Gilligan! He done either layed down on the play (situation) or tripped out, not really trying to get involved with the festivities. Here it is though, you were willing and ready to go balls out and press with and representing what you're representing (city and turf).

Just b'cuz it looks like it, dress like it, or act like it, don't mean it's it! (SMH) Trust though, dudes do fly up under the radar and you will never know until that fucked up situation comes about, but it always happens like that. It might be too late then, that's a dude playing with the game and horseplaying. Be mindful though, it's going to cost you, playing with what dudes lost homies behind and lose homies behind. I can say, you do have to know who you're fucking with, surrounded by and the page they're on. I get it's hard, due the illusion factor, that Penn and Teller shit, that illusion of truth again wearing that mask of deception. That's how dudes are able to fly up under the radar. Another thing to be mindful of, dudes aren't stupid enough to do shit, they're just arrogant enough to do it.

I truly hope everything I've said resonated with you or can resonate with you. I can only hope to be overstood though, as only I could be. Being the overstanding is as it is with me, for what I know and overstand it to be, thus giving it to you. My overstanding what a niggah signed up for isn't what a niggah signed up for...not at all! But don't take my word for it though. Shoot your shot if that's what it's going to take for you to get your mind around it and for you to feel it. I get it, there's nothing like learning, knowing and overstanding something as only it is and can be, with and for you... Yeah, I know, I have the worst case of the fuck its!

# Chapter 8

## "Somebody Have To Learn The Hard Way"

Let me start, though, by saying you don't have to learn the hard way when you can actually get a bar without getting a bar, learning from the next dude that's been through it or have experienced it or have been exposed to it. Cried for that same instance, bled for that same instance, rode for that same instance, dude's been banged and bagged for that same instance, a dude ain't trying to tell you what to do, or none of that type of shit. A dude just isn't trying to see dudes "wrecking" (being in harm's way) as they so often do, "DTM" (doing too much) and too much of the wrong thing (shenanigans, Gilliganism, etc.) and I can bang that! It's never about a dude trying to tell a dude what to do, but shit, if I have something that I feel is of value, why not put it in the air, for sure. I'm all about and for learn, know and overstand. It took me to learn, know and overstand the hard way.

Sometimes it takes that, b'cuz dudes just don't get it and don't seem to get it (SMH). I wish now, I didn't go through what a mutha fucka did to get it right. I took myself through thee ringer fucking around with the fuck around! Going against the grain and constantly bumping my head, at almost every turn, like dayum, something has to give or let up around this mutha fucka! I was pretty much making it up as I went along, that's why a lot of the results were the same. It was like I was doing the same shit but hoping for different results. That wasn't what the reality of it was though, not by a long shot. Everything happens for a reason though, I'm a firm believer in that sentiment. If a dudes telling you the "whore bag" that stays down the block is a "turf rat" and she's fucking this, that or the other homie and she burnt them and had their shit smoking (dick). Why would you go behind them and fuck her nasty ass without a rubber? (SMH) ...That's out!

That's just fucking retarded. Dude told you the bitch is burning dudes and you still pull up on her. Like a dude was lying to you to keep you from trying to fuck (SMH). So how that work out for you? Oh, you just had to see for yourself if that pussy was on fire huh? Couldn't take my word for it though huh? This bitch is running around setting fires, burning dudes' dicks (SMH). No bueno! Won't get tic! How about you meet a bitch and she stays in enemigo turf and you tell a homie you're about to slide through and fuck with her and he says to you, "Cuz, that ain't a good look, kick back on that." But you go anyway and niggahs trip on you, you end up feeling some type of way, going back through tripping! Yeah, she said dudes were bitches and busters, this, that and the third and whatever else she said to you about them. You told the homie and he's still going to tell you, "It ain't a good look!" On some real shit, you can't listen to no bitch when it comes to that type of shit, her info is Mickey, a bitch will say anything and tell you what you want to hear, plus that's how she may see them but who the fuck is she? You can't ever take her word on that, though, it'll quickly go bluey bluey. A'ight, bitches and busters. You definitely can't listen to that bitch homie. She's pumping a dude up for failure. A bitch will tell a dude what she thinks he wants to hear, quick fast

## FEELING SOME TYPE OF WAY—SODO AUSTIN

and in a hurry, if it's fitting her equation. (SMH) That's just keeping it a hunnid with you, straight up!

Gon and take your ass over there though, if you want to. Your mind's set, a dude can't talk to you or talk you out of it. Peace Black Man, sag it out then. You're going to fuck around and test the water, fucking with what that bitch talking about and find yourself banged, whupped out or bagged (SMH) listening to that bitch, period on that type of shit. It's a game to them. You're the one who's going to take that ride though, on some goofball ass shit! Me being Bitterchild advocate, handle your wax if that's your look...do you! It's always a lesson to be learned from it, it's never a game homie. But yeah, a dude's homie know it can and get Mickey with that whole situation.

You're basically a liability. Dudes just aren't going to leave you. What does that look like, no matter how Mickey it is? But if they do "do it moving on you" (leave you) and something were to happen to you, they have an issue coming (a DP). It doesn't matter if you got banged or not, dudes still have that coming, for "stage lefting" on you. How the fuck homies are just going to leave you for dead? Riddle me that! But you know, you'll always have homies that will shoot their shot (SMH) and find out the hard way. At the end of the day, homies aren't just going to bounce on you and dip (leave). Someone will try to get to you and get you out of harm's way of the bussing, which puts them in harm's way, putting their safety at risk of being banged or bagged along with you, b'cuz you're on the block or in the turf wet. So the thing was, you get caught like that, that's a DP. The homie Baldie a few weeks after that call was made was

## FEELING SOME TYPE OF WAY—SODO AUSTIN

DP'ed for it (being in the turf wet). So anyway, the G homie was just left like that. Had I not been out and posted, there's no telling what could've happened to the homie. He was wet...stupidly wet! He most definitely shouldn't have been out there like that.

Enemigo would've and could've had at the homie, he was faded as fuck. I'm just glad the shit worked out the way it did and not the other way b'cuz it could've went ugly and they were out riding around looking to bag something, thinking they had them one. I spot enemigo on 20th and King, me and the G homie were a few houses down from the corner where enemigo sat. They drove past us, I guess they decided they had "vics" (victims) b'cuz they went to the next corner (21st and King) and "flipped a dick" (a U-turn) and came back. Before they made it back through, I had had my .40 out and ready to go as we were standing there. We had turned to face the street and the approaching swoop and I had the .40 visible in my right hand. As they approached us, I kind of raised the .40. They just looked at me, the homie and the smoker. I kept the .40 visible until they passed, mugging them the whole time. The passenger just nodded at us, but they kept moving. I nodded back like "Not tonight, cuz!" You're doing no shining around here (SMH). The swoop made a right on 20th and King, going towards Atlantic. Had I not been there on the block posted that night trying to get some work off, the homie probably could've been "aired out" (shot), no doubt in my mind. He was easy pickings. He knew he shouldn't have been out there like that, based on that type of shit happening. In his defense though, it wasn't on him, but still it would've been a fucked up lesson to learn the hard way and at his expense. We chopped it up though (talked), later the next morning. Every day for a few weeks, we had started meeting up in the turf on the block to chop it up and blow a blunt, then we would part ways for the day.

He asked me though, to keep that situation under my hat, which I did. I never exposed the situation though. Truth be told, though, I was more tripping off of who the G homie was with than him actually being wet in the turf, b'cuz that was fucked up and they horseplayed with the homie's life. (SMH) Bullshit ass niggahs! They just let the homie out of the swoop and smashed off (drove off). All I'm saying is, they could've made sure the homie got in the yard safely. Instead of just letting him out in that type of condition and on the opposite side of the street. That's just foul. Had I not had that banger, we were all hollered at. The smoker would've got it on some "You fucking with them, you ducking with them" type shit. Moving along, that's like a dude telling you not to go to this certain liquor store, but you're like, "Fuck that, I'm going anyway," and it's "bluey bluey!" Why bump your head against the brick wall and don't have to, when you saw the next dude do it? It's like a dude isn't satisfied until something jump off (happen) or it goes bluey bluey!

It appears a dude's word ain't never good enough for the most part. Why does something have to go sideways for a dude to get it or get a clue, or for a dude to believe that fat meat is greasy? There's no "reverse" button, no "hold up" button, no "pause" button, no "start over" button or "do over" button and sometimes there's no "get back" from learning the hard way. It's going to be a dude saying he learned the hard way, but in reality, you hadn't learned shit b'cuz you're out of here, they're speaking

## FEELING SOME TYPE OF WAY—SODO AUSTIN

past tense. Learning something is actually learning from the situation and moving forward, not repeating it. A lot of shit dudes do it's always an easier way, but which one sounds better to you? You don't always have to take the hard way. Why not just learn from the next dude's situation?

We don't know how the fuck we got where we were, let alone where he came from, but he was "wet" (high as fuck). Anyway, we're talking and posted up by a wall. The homie walked by the bus stop where another homie was sitting on the bench. I guess he was going to talk to the homie, but got distracted by the bus pulling up, then stopped to let passengers exit and enter. The back door of the bus opened and an Ese was standing by the backdoor. The homie "fired his shit up" (hit him). All you heard was "Orrrdaaalay!" The Ese just looked at the homie like he'd lost his mind, like: "What the fuck you hit me for nigger!" He didn't say that verbally but if you could've read his face (SMH), the homie was every nigger in the book. The backdoor closed and the bus pulled off. About 30 minutes go by. We were still in that same parking lot bullshitting and talking.

A couple of homegirls pulled up in a "smoker's bucket" (a crackhead's hooptie). Me and three of the homies step to the bucket and start talking to them. The homie Stretch, who was wet and fired on the Ese was now standing at the entrance of the parking lot talking to another homie and pointing to another homie or appeared to be. A brown eighty something Toyota pulled up in the street on the other side of the end of the parking lot at the other entrance. The same Ese the homie had fired on hopped out of the swoop from the back passenger side door. We were all

## FEELING SOME TYPE OF WAY—SODO AUSTIN

faded (high and drunk) as fuck, but we're off of the weed and liquor. We didn't really pay all that much attention to who he was (the Ese). He just pretty much walked past us at the swoop. I turned and looked briefly at him though, but still hadn't focused on him. I just saw an Ese. He wasn't banged out (dressed like a banger) or nothing, so I didn't deem him a threat and basically dismissed him. Clearly he was a threat and on a mission.

    Me and the other homie looked at him, turning back around, continuing fucking with the homegirls and talking to them. The next thing we know we're hearing a scuffle and a commotion. We all turn around. The Ese's on top of the homie with 2 ten inch butcher knives, trying to buss (stab) on the homie and was really trying to do damage. Another homie that was much closer to the situation rushed and tackled the Ese to get him up off of the homie. Once he was off the homie, knives on the ground and being off of his feet, he jumped the fuck up quick and got in the wind. We gave chase, chasing him and running in and out of traffic. The Ese managed to jump into the back of a pickup truck in the bed of it. Somehow he pulls out a third butcher knife and was slashing and swinging it at us b'cuz we had the bed surrounded, trying to get him off of his feet. Mind you the truck was sitting at the traffic light. As soon as the light changed, that mutha fucka pulls off and was out of there (SMH). We watched it get little, standing in the middle of the street, before swoops started coming.

    I don't know how the homie didn't get served, it was clearly an "All praise is due to Allah, to Allah we belong and to Him we return" moment.

## FEELING SOME TYPE OF WAY—SODO AUSTIN

The homie was a wrap...whaaat! He only suffered a minor wound to the bottom of his foot through his shoe. The niggah was blessed as fuck, real talk, just wasn't his time to go (die). You can't call none of that lucky. Luck has nothing to do with it, that was all Allah! How that Ese was jabbing, poking and stabbing at the homie, to a mutha fucka looking at it from a distance or even up close, it looked like he was going hard on the homie, doing his shit, suuuper! The Ese didn't do any damage other than that small cut on the bottom of the homies foot. But yeah, you would've swore up and down he was bagging the homie. What was crazy, didn't nobody have a banger (SMH). Shit, Allah was looking out for the both of them. Really looking out for the homie, he was covered, based on though.

That whole situation was Mickey as fuck. Like wow, did this shit just really happen, cuz! Horseplaying, the young homie could've really been bagged, fucking around on that Gilligan shit! All behind a niggah being high and wanting to fuck with somebody (SMH). You know the adage: "A hard head will make a soft ass!" Every time. Like an instance where I was talking about a G homie. He didn't fuck with nobody in the sense of fucking with them, trying to fuck over them or do something to them, real cool dude. Anyway, some other homies, basically left the G homie for dead, leaving him in the state he was in, off the water and in the middle of the street, some cold niggahs (SMH).

They could've let the homie out of the swoop on the same side of the street the house he was going to was on, instead of where they let him out on, which was the opposite side. At the end of the day, they could've walked him across (SMH) instead of just leaving the homie like that,

## FEELING SOME TYPE OF WAY—SODO AUSTIN

which wasn't cool! Be mindful, we have a "no fly zone" in the turf. That alone should've been the reason they, whoever they were, should've made sure the homie went in the house or at least inside the yard. Homies know that homies aren't supposed to be walking around the turf like that or being in the turf period wet. B'cuz not only are you jeopardizing homies, but you're jeopardizing yourself. Homies b'cuz they have to make sure you're straight, if something were to happen or enemigo pull up bussing! If mutha fuckas were to pull up in a swoop and started bussing, you can't really function that way you need to, or how you normally do or can. Everything is off as far as your faculties and you're on some Matrix type shit. (SMH)

    By homies living where we lived, it drew other homies to come through and hang out on the block (60th and Linden/61st and Linden). A lot of shit went on and stayed happening though, based on who we were and where we were from, Eastside Insane Crip (BG's, Youngs and Babyz). A Young homie got shot in the left ass cheek. Another instance, me and a few Young homies were standing on 60th and Atlantic on the corner talking, waiting for the light to change to green, and a red Nissan passed us up with the passenger hanging out of the window, letting off a single shot...bloom! Fuck bugs! But these bitch ass dudes couldn't have been no killahs. Not only didn't dude doing the bussing hit nobody, but the swoop didnt stop and nobody tried hopping out to handle their B.I. It was no bueno on that play. I myself knew better than to be hanging in that area without a banger but occasionally I did and just left it at the house. Cold thing about it, it could've been anybody. You have a lot of dudes from

## FEELING SOME TYPE OF WAY—SODO AUSTIN

everywhere living on the North Side...from everywhere, from L.A. to Compton. We've had run ins with dudes from both demographics. From that day on though, I stayed strapped fucking around there, I kept it. But yeah, they had us "dead bang" (dead to rights) being posted as we were on the corner like that...straight targets! (SMH) Didn't hit shit! Truly an all praise is due to Allah, to Allah we belong and to Him do we return moment.

    The weirdo dudes could've been no more than three fucking feet away from us and he only "get off" (shot) once. Initially, it sounded like a swoop back firing...blup blup bop! I didn't really trip off what happened until the dude was leaning out of the window dissing the turf. Then it registered what happened...bitch ass niggahs! We were feeling some type of way. For the most part, it was my wake up call. I was straight on all of the Gilligan shit. After I left, the same Young homies were running around in the same area doing the same shit and one of them bagged the Young homie Baby CJ (I.I.P.), the G homie Big CJ's nephew. There was a young homegirl named Queena, my niggah Big Dan Dog's cuzzo. She stayed "popping fish grease" (had a disrespectful mouth), talking sideways and talking shit basically. One night though, her and some lil homies were at my spot blowing and drinking and they left late, heading to the homie NSK Day's spot, who went by Small Day Day.

    I hear some bussing at a distance while I'm in my room with situation who had talked me out of leaving, going with them. She basically was in her feelings and talking shit, so I "fell back" (didn't leave). The next morning, though, I found out it was them who'd gotten bussed on, after they'd left my spot. One of the homies had gotten banged. That was the homie I was saying took "one" (slug) to the left ass cheek. "She" on the other hand (Queena) was banged in the face. She ended up being straight though (SMH). Her whole demeanor changed after that, she calmed that shit the fuck down (her energy). I don't know if it was her that had gotten them bussed on, running her mouth or if it was just enemigos spotting the young homies, being gang gang, got at them. Either instance, I know she said something, it wouldn't be her not to. Keeping it a hunnid though. She did get some "act right" about herself, that's what the fuck she did do, most definitely...whaaat!

Like with this instance where I've previously spoke on a situation with me and the homie Big Pint "being wet" (under the influence of PCP) behind his apartment complex, when the Ese pulled back up on us (me and him) bussing and the homie dropped like he got banged. All along though, it was him using war tactics (play dead) (SMH). That's out, fucking with me! The niggah was laid out a few steps away from where the swoop sat and the Ese was bussing. The whole time I was being bussed at he wasn't moving at all. Me and probably ole boy too (the Ese) thought he bagged Pint, that illusion of truth wearing that mask of deception well is a mutha fucka! Eastside! He's a braver niggah than me though, that would've never happened with me. But yeah, Pint shot a cold illusion out there (SMH). Sherm will have you sometimes thinking outside of the box (SMH). My nuts don't drag like that, not by a long shot! ...Whaaat! On some real shit though, me, I wouldn't have got on the ground playing dead...that was no bueno! Nah, I wasn't going to be able to do it, that's out! Just a few feet

## FEELING SOME TYPE OF WAY—SODO AUSTIN

away (SMH). If dude would've decided to open the swoop door, he'd have been standing on top of the homie. That's how close to the homie he was, if that Ese were gang gang or just active period, he would've gotten out of the swoop, making sure the homie was bagged. Me being a Bitterchild advocate again, that shit could've went real sideways for the homie, horseplaying. He's playing bagged and could've really got bagged. What was the lesson? Riddle me that. Fucking with a dude who isn't fucking with you and he came back and hollered like, yeah, "I ain't him homie!" He tried to do his stuff on niggahs. Another homie do the same type of Gilligan shit, suuuper! And off of the water. It's about 5 to 8 homies in this Mexican market parking lot talking. Everybody was off trees and drink. The homie just popped up out of the sky.

    That's why homie's saying what the fuck he's saying. It's not for his health dude! Nine out of ten he's pulling up on you b'cuz he'd been there and done that, being thirsty on some dick and pussy shit! And damn near got bagged, banged or whupped out! Yeah, one of those, "All praise is due to Allah, to Allah we belong and to Him we return" moments, behind a whore bag and her pussy. She'll say anything to get a dude to bite, to get him to pull up to her spot, especially if a dude is showing any type of reluctance, promising a dude the world. "Just come through, I'm going to do this, that and the third to the dick...I'm going to let you do this, that and the third to the pussy...we're going to do this, that and the third." That bad look isn't resonating at all! (SMH) Again, dudes aren't stupid enough to do something. I come to learn and overstand they're arrogant enough, with no regard. The pain I feel still isn't exclusive, living a little, dying a lot. You know yourself, you shouldn't go, but you do anyway on the case of the fuck its! B'cuz you're trying "to hit" (have sex).

But shit, most dudes shoot their shot. I've done it a gang of times, messing with a whore bag. Looking back and seeing it for what it is, I was playing with the game and taking it for granted, leaving myself open to get banged, bagged or whupped out! Being a Gilligan, horseplaying. Another instance, you know "Task Force" is out tough in the turf every Tuesday and they're hopping out on dudes, running up on them, but you're still trying to "serve" (sell) your work or get off a few sacks of bud or dip a few sticks. Dude, if you don't knock it the fuck off (SMH). It's going to take you to be sitting in the backseat of "The Ones" (police) swoop to figure it out b'cuz thirst and common sense isn't doing it for you But then again, from what I'm seeing, common sense isn't so common nowadays. So yeah, it's going to take you to go to jail to realize you shouldn't be serving anything on Tuesdays and Thursdays.

Yeah, I forgot about Thursdays. How many homies you've seen or know that was caught up fucking around? Dudes know "Task Force" and the "Gang Unit" be on one and stay pushing. How about you're pushing in the turf and knowing enemigo is running around or just out and about, doing what they do, and you're not strapped, yet steady pushing around in their turf slipping. Slipping b'cuz that's what you're doing not being strapped or security conscious. Why make your career shorter and come to an end faster than it's supposed to? Due to you being on some Gilligan shit! Being hardheaded. We know the outcome, we know the results,

## FEELING SOME TYPE OF WAY—SODO AUSTIN

they're imminent since you want to "throw rocks" outside of the penitentiary (SMH) or "kick rocks" in the graveyard (SMH). The homies done told you, enemigos are lurking, looking to holler at any homie they can, gang gang or not and they're riding around in the turf three deep, trying to catch anyone slipping. East Side!

On some anybody's out type shit, they're going to basically be a victim and can cancel Christmas, their "born day" and cancel some more shit! So to make you feel my pain and make you a believer, you have to get banged or whupped out, laid the fuck out in the street or on the sidewalk. If you're bagged, it really doesn't matter does it? B'cuz you've learned the ultimate lesson. You don't have to be a believer, you were made one...feeling your last pain! I've personally had a few young homies who've hung out like that on a daily on the North Side of "The City" (Long Beach).

For one, this isn't even our side of the City. We're off the East Side, and mind you, we beef (my turf) with everything that isn't Asian or Samoan/Tungan. So everything on the North Side are enemigos at the end of the day. 4 Corner Blocks, O-Hoods, Brick Boys, Blvd's, Mac Mafias, North Side Longos and anybody else who has beef with the turf on that side. The young homies though, would run around all willy-nilly, with no banger for the most part. With no banger and they're getting into it with dudes from off the North and with Ese's. A couple of times somebody came through bussing (shooting) but didn't hit none of the young homies, not even the main young homie that was gang gang, out there "knocking

## FEELING SOME TYPE OF WAY—SODO AUSTIN

shit down" (catching bodies). You kept hearing him. Bloom! Bloom! Bloom! He kept it hot! He's all bad now though. Lil niggah made a statement on a homie from "Youngs" about a "hot topic" (murder). Everywhere he pulled up in the maze on a yard, homies are on him like back pockets, he's catching the greys. (SMH)

He's been voted off the island, but he refuses to take his batteries out. His career, though, is "throu'vo" (through...finished...done...finito!) But yeah, the young homies stayed in the same area we hung around in. I stayed a block or 2 away. Where we stayed was pretty much the turf away from the turf b'cuz a lot of homies lived in, near or around the area, pulling up and hanging out. Even East Side homies would pull up.

Especially peeping (seeing) the outcome isn't straight and it being what it is. We already know how dudes are always saying shit like, "Just b'cuz it happened like that with them don't mean it's going to happen like that with me." (SMH) Riddle me this, though, champ. What makes you the exception? But you're right, I can give you that: just b'cuz shit happened and went crooked for them doesn't mean it's going to play out the same way or have that same outcome with you. "They got banged, you get banged." ..."They got away and was told on, you were caught dead bang." It can go way worse for you. Its like I said, there's a way you can hit a lick (rob) that you can get your rabbs and get away, based on my doing it another way before and getting wrapped the fuck up, learning the hard way, bluey bluey. If a dude is telling you, "Aye, it ain't straight homie, it ain't a go, fall back." It must not be straight, the go ain't a go (SMH). I'm sure a mutha fucka isn't going out of his way to say something that isn't

## FEELING SOME TYPE OF WAY—SODO AUSTIN

straight or something isn't a go just to be saying it or say it isn't straight to be trying to get off of some work on the block if it isn't straight!

That's wasted energy. What is a dude getting out of that? Where is he coming up in that scenario? Riddle me that. Or saying it's not straight, trying to hit something that's been hit and dudes got wrapped up or caught up every time. A dude will tell you, "Nah cuz, that ain't straight, niggahs stay caught up fucking with that, look that way!" Do you listen though, or take heed to that advice? Hell nah! Now look where you're at though. How is it working out for you? I was thinking about an instance where I lost a homie from the turf. He had "hit a lick" (robbed). He got some Jamaicans for some work and some rabbs. The Jamaicans knew who the homie was and knew who his family was, based on the family being a known family. They gave the homie a pass basically and chalked it up to the game, them being caught slipping and accepting it for what it was. The homie went back and tried to get these same Jamaicans...again! Whaaat!

He fucked around and met a very pernicious ending. They bagged the homie (SMH). He misconstrued them not tripping for a second time, that just wasn't the reality of it. Not only did the homie come back, but he got fly and brought some other homies with him. The lesson there being, you don't try to jack the same mutha fuckas you already jacked, especially under the circumstances surrounding it...you horseplayed and it went bluey bluey! Though the homie didn't learn from the lesson itself, maybe the next niggah can. For the homie there's no "do overs" or "start overs." It's a wrap. The homie was a childhood homie, stayed a few blocks away. I stayed on 20th and Cerritos, he was on 21st and Olive. The homie went

## FEELING SOME TYPE OF WAY—SODO AUSTIN

out backwards. I mean, that's just something a niggah shouldn't have tried fucking with. You've been there and done that, it was a wrap. I don't know what the homie read into it b'cuz they accepted it and chalked it up, but whatever it was he read into it was a wrong read. Wasn't nothing good coming out of that Mickey situation...not at all!

Either a dude was going to get banged the fuck up, no if, ands, or buts about it. You couldn't possibly think that wouldn't come out crooked or go sideways. Jacking a dude and then going back to do it again, if you don't knock it the fuck off! A dude is already feeling some type of way and here you come (SMH). Are you serious...are you fucking for real? I wonder if anybody told the homie that wouldn't be a good look and to fall back (leave it alone). 9 out of 10, I doubt it, but who's to say? For all a niggah know niggahs might've been telling the homie, "Hell yeah. Fuck it cuz. The Maicans gave it up once, they gon run that back again!" They did give it up too. Bloom, bloom, bloom, blop, blop, blop, bloom, bloom! Multiple rounds. If I jacked a niggah and got away, that's a wrap, it's over with. Horseplaying by going back, that's no bueno! I don't give a fuck how easy it was or how quick they gave it up, I'm straight, suuuper straight!

That can go so crooked b'cuz if you jack a niggah or niggahs you know and they know where you be and you don't bag their ass, they can pull back up on you. That's where the hard way comes in. The easy thing to do is just bag that ass and be done with it. The hard way is not bagging a niggah, giving them action at getting back. What do you learn? You learn that if you jack a mutha fucka and they know where they can pull up on you at, they're inspired, they're going to run that play, and why wouldn't

## FEELING SOME TYPE OF WAY—SODO AUSTIN

they? But by not bagging them, you're leaving a left door wide open to be bagged or even banged. Basically, you left yourself exposed to be got. How's that for the hard way for a niggah's ass? That's just the reality of it though. If a homie say, "Cuz, I ain't feeling the block, it's too hot, it's too quiet, something don't feel right, I'm about to bounce, you coming?"

Technically, that's your "Q" to bounce but you stay though. You stay but he bounces and thirty minutes later the Ones hit the block thick, and you and the homies get "gaffled" (arrested). Or some enemigos come through "getting off" (shooting) and somebody gets bagged. The homie said something didn't feel right, but I guess niggahs had to see what he meant instead of bouncing too and shit got Mickey. A homie saying to you don't go to this bitch's house b'cuz it's not straight. One, it's in enemigo turf and you're on a block where these dudes post on, on a daily. Morning, noon and night, somebody is posted on the block. It's a hangout and two, it's her homies. The argument is if shit got Mickey, who do you think she's going to side with or protect? You or her homies? Basically, dudes she came up with, knew forever, more than likely fucked a few of them. It damn sure isn't going to be you. She's from over there and grew up with most of them. If not all of them. Not only that, she has to live around there "H.O.N." (homies over niggahs) anyway. She might talk shit, but that's all she's going to do. She's just going to watch her homies beat the brakes off you! She's definitely not going to interfere or try to stop shit and you're assed out! Real talk. It's not like she could've helped you anyway. If she wanted to, bitch only a hunnid pounds (SMH). Yeah, it ain't a good look, but the homie told you that already though. It ain't like you didn't know the possibilities of being tripped on were. I guess you had to check that look out for yourself huh? A niggah's trying to put you up on the Mickey shit so you don't wreck or fall victim to the shenanigans. A niggah's not going to ever steer you wrong.

I'm not that bullshit homie I've spoke on! I'm not ever trying to see a dude wreck fucking around on some Gilligan shit, it's just as real as that. I'm straight personally with learning from the next dude's mistakes and downfalls now. But you know, it came after I learned shit the hard way. If it's an easier route or another way to be took, I'm with that, please believe it. If I peep (see) a niggah bump his head, why do I want to come behind him and bump mine? It makes no sense when I peeped him bump his. The whole thing is, if it's an easier route or better way, that's what the B.I. is. Fuck doing shit the hard way when a niggah don't have to get it like that. For what? When you don't have to and you were shown that that wasn't straight. Especially if a niggah can peep the obvious. That's something that didn't work for the next niggah or that last niggah. Like yeah, "I won't be getting it like that, that's out!" It was exposed as the wrong way and the wrong route, so that isn't the B.I. I'm going to leave there on that note though.

# Chapter 9

## "G Homies"

G homies are basically that, much older homies that have been around and had a hand in paving the way for those who came behind him. Older homies that created the tone for the turf by way of politics, whether on the streets or in the pen. For the most part, they played by their own rules from my experience and will be on some "Do as I say, not as I do" type shit. Game recognotice game. That's on some other type shit, manipulating situations and manipulating homies to the point it's only fitting their equation. If you're going to lead through shit and see it for what and as it is, you're going to become the victim of politics that's not about you but about a bigger captured moment. I advise homies not to play into the G homie politics b'cuz nobody's going to lose but you. You're going to be on the losing end of that look, and I can bang that. Some, not all, would be on some "Do as I do" type shit, as in "What applies to you don't apply to me, what applies to me don't apply to you!"

As I said, G homies be on some Mickey shit...can be, do be. "I'm exempt from you, this, that and the third, you can challenge me if you want to though," meant just that (SMH), especially being gang gang, easily going bluey bluey! You just know not to "play that game" (cross that line) when it comes to certain G homies that play ball and does play ball. Some, though, will have you thinking it's gravity but in reality it's far from gravity. G homie is tripping, just waiting for that right place and time to press play. G homies can be sneaky as fuck, especially the gang gang

## FEELING SOME TYPE OF WAY—SODO AUSTIN

ones that are still getting their hands dirty and staying in traffic. Don't let them fool you, they politic and are with the shit. Stay tied and connected to the young homies that are gang gang. So you have to always be careful around certain homies and watch what comes out of your mouth...just saying! You have to also be mindful of the fact that G homies always have ears and eyes in the turf, from all generations. They're always kept in the loop.

Homies will wonder how G homies know certain shit about certain shit that was said or went on. If you didn't know, now you do. They always have young homies under their thumbs, just for that reason. They stay informed and they stay in traffic, they're involved with the turf. At the end of the day they have sympathizers and they stay moving about in the turf. Get a bar! Makes no sense, you do have G homies with good intentions. You have them with bad ones playing dirty politics, playing the manipulation game or playing off their rep of being gang gang. Being known for what they do, how they do it and for what they've done, using that fear element as well to their advantage. You have those G homies that'll use their G status for Mickey shit in the turf, suuuper! For personal reasons and gain, them on what they're on. Those that sympathize with them, let me clarify that. These are usually, too, younger homies who think they're above the law in the turf. B'cuz of the support behind them and certain G homies, thinking they're untouchable! ...Whaaat! I've been around and have functioned with good G homies, solid G homies, with nothing but the best intentions for a younger homie and for the turf. And will be feeling some type of way when other G homies don't have them.

## FEELING SOME TYPE OF WAY—SODO AUSTIN

I've been around G homies too that were on that Mickey shit and always on that Mickey shit. I fucked with them, but I didn't fuck with them if they weren't my cup of tea. I wasn't on what they were on. I'm sure I wasn't their cup of tea either b'cuz they knew I couldn't be manipulated and wasn't just going to fall in with their crowd of homies and conform.

I do have my G homies I have major love and respect for. I have my G homies I have love for and G homies I have respect for. I didn't do scandalous, I didn't do plot on homies, I didn't do fuck over homies, I didn't jack homies, wasn't my get down. I didn't fuck with the Mickey shit when it came to homies in the turf. I fucked with the homies, I fucked with the turf and about both...and gang gang! Loved the turf, loved the homies, loved the homie'ism, loved what I signed up for, pushed and represented to the best of my ability. I loved it even when it didn't love me or have love for me. I represented and pushed not just for me but for my homies and for the turf. Respected all of my G homies, those that earned it and deserved it. Those that didn't, I didn't disrespect them, I just limited myself when it came to being in their presence, limiting my conversation to certain topics I didn't get into anything that was of significance, I didn't engage either way.

I just kept things simple and kept it cordial, based on the homie factor. As for G homies, I don't knock them or downplay their status, b'cuz at the end of the day their still "G homie" whether I feel he's bullshit or not, that's just what it is. But could he have sent me on a mission? No bueno! Could he have got me to side with him on some shit? No bueno! Could he have got me to turn on another G homie? No bueno! You're a G

## FEELING SOME TYPE OF WAY—SODO AUSTIN

homie but not that G homie! You're the same G homie other G homies half ass fuck with and respect...will get disrespected in a heartbeat, knowing who other homies don't know. The same G homie that's not in the turf like that or come to meetings (SMH). Let's address the elephant in the room. G homies who've done some things...yeah, done some rat bastard shit!

But kept in the dark by other G homies (SMH), for whatever reasons and allowing young homies to fuck with you (SMH). What baffles me, you're still in the turf or come around (SMH). I've been around G homies that other G homies really weren't feeling or didn't feel, just basically tolerated them. Based on how they got down, get down or have gotten down. The type of G homie that if he were to come up bagged, niggahs really wouldn't give a fuck or would be tripping off of it, based on his Mickiness. It would be left as it is, what it is, and with no repercussions, with not too much talk about it afterwards either. Just being one of those things where saying little or nothing is saying a lot. But niggahs are going to the funeral, no doubt. It's what niggahs do regardless. Homies mounting up, going to the funeral with homie's face on a T-shirt... East Side! The only ones who would probably be feeling some type of way or give a fuck are those who were on the same shit they were on and fucked with him/them on whatever page the fucked around on.

Of course, they're going to be on some "emo" shit and feeling some type of way. That's to be expected, feeling as though they've lost one of their own. Anything less would be a mis-overstanding. As I've said, though, I've been around good G homies with genuine intentions, trying to guide and steer younger homies right and in the right direction, not trying to have them or see them wreck. I've had good conversations with them too, about the life and the state of it, as a whole, as it is today, with all the dirty shit and underhanded shit at play. The different ways it's presented, having a presence. They were Mickey and laced me on how to recognotice certain shit that comes out of dudes' mouth and taking shit with a grain of sand, it's not all that it seems. Laced me on how to see and navigate through the bullshit when it's being shot from a mutha fucka, trying to shoot their shot (SMH).

Some of it is transparent as fuck though, easily read. So a lot of what I know and have come to overstand came from G homies, that didn't want to see a young niggah misled or tainted from bad teachings and misguided guidance. Having a bad overstanding of what it was to bang or be a good homie. I had started really seeing shit from a different perspective, from what and as it was from fucking with my G niggahs. As I sat back and started analyzing shit they would do, how they moved, things they would say, some do and did have homies' best interest at heart, as I'd come to overstand. But a lot of them were on some Mickey shit and still are, especially with manipulation, they play that game good as fuck (SMH), for sure they play ball on that.

How they would and do manipulate situations with homies in the turf, it's like dudes are being moved about like chess pieces, even amongst other G homies. As a younger homie from the turf, fucking with them too much, they'll come to expect you to ride with them and side with them and side with them when shit's internal with homies. You're expected to choose sides when it's internal. That could be a Mickey situation, depending on the G homie. The coldest shit I've come to find out was how G homies from a turf and a G homie from an enemigo turf would work together on some rabb shit, in the middle of a heated beef, using each other's younger homies to clear out an area or block where rabbs are being made, b'cuz they're "booming" (prosperous and heavy trafficked) (SMH) on some Mickey shit. I'm gon tell you where or how to send your lil homies to buss in my turf and you tell me where to send my lil homies to buss. No one's none the wiser (SMH). Then they'll send lil homies they fuck with in the area or on that block. But not until after the bussing they created die down and their homies aren't hanging on that block or in the area (SMH).

That's a cold game to be playing, but they done it. Cold games are played, I've seen that played out on more that 2 occasions. They're the biggest politicians in the turf, suuuper! Politickers on the highest of levels and are bullshit dudes. Don't think nothing goes on in the turf for the most part the G homies don't know about when it come to shit going on in the turf, those that are gang gang and have a presence. G homies you see in the turf day in and day out, out and on the block. You see them posted, functioning. You see them at meetings and at functions, basically functioning. These are the G homies that are visible and are the ones younger homies are respecting and are fucking with. You can be a G homie, but if you're not functional, aren't visible or have a presence, younger homies aren't giving you that love or respect as a G homie. Not giving a fuck about who you used to run with, none of that.

## FEELING SOME TYPE OF WAY—SODO AUSTIN

If that's not you now, you don't have a voice. Young homies aren't hearing you and aren't trying to hear you, or feel you. Their thing is why should they listen to or hear a niggah that's not functional or gang gang and will let you know they aren't feeling you or what you're talking about, don't have no respect coming whatsoever... East Side! Can a dude be a G homie and really expect a young homie to do some shit he's not doing? Young homies are respecting G homies that are pushing and still active! Gang gang or about something that has to do with the turf or the homie when you don't have a presence or are one? It's the same shit when niggahs are in the maze (prison). Really not a presence when the beef is on. You're not anywhere to be seen or heard from, a straight ghost.

But you feel you have an input about something. If you don't knock it off! From that standpoint, I can overstand how young homie's feeling some type of way and not feeling you. Different ball game in the maze, you have no choice but to be functional and be a presence. It's the same with me, I respect and have love for all of my G homies that are present as far as having a presence and have one, functioning and still gang gang. I can see myself hearing them and listening to them, based on. They're doing what I'm doing, they're in the dark on a daily, like I'm in the turf on a daily and still in the turf when the beef's cracking. Though a G homie acts like he just got it like that off the dribble, like he got that coming and a dude supposed to just give him that respect...no bueno! Acting like a young homie just supposed to move b'cuz he says move. Stop horseplaying!

## FEELING SOME TYPE OF WAY—SODO AUSTIN

Are you moving? Fuck nah! Are you out there in the field, in the thick of it? Fuck nah, you ain't! The G homies I trip off the most though, are the one's that been in the maze and out of the way for a lot of years, then come back and just think homies are going to march to their drumbeat or supposed to march to their drumbeat. Come on now, this shit isn't nowhere near like it was when you were out there. I'm quite sure niggahs are coming in and out telling you that the turf isn't the same, telling you what's going on. You got it stuck in your head you're going to get out and try to tell niggahs what they're going to do or aren't going to do...whaaat! Niggah, you're horseplaying! What's going to happen or isn't going to happen, if you don't knock it off. How you're going to change this, that and the third (SMH). What you're going to do is find yourself in a Mickey situation, found somewhere bagged, real talk. That's a game dudes shouldn't be playing or trying to play, especially when homies have told you it's not going to happen that way. Hard heads make for niggahs bagged! Don't take my word for it though. But yeah, keeping it one hunnid, them young dudes don't know you, don't give a fuck about you, what you're going through or who you think you are or used to be.

Yeah, they may have heard of you and respect your past "get down" as far as your gang gang, but all of that is over with, done with, dunzo. So why are you bringing up old shit? I personally had to get at the G homie Rocc Head (What Up Mark Hall) that been down since the early 80's, '82 or '83 somewhere around there. I'm hearing he's out now as of 2021. Anyway, we talked about this very shit. He was one of the G homies that had it stuck in his head that he's going to get out and regulate some shit (SMH).

I told the G homie off the dribble that that wasn't going to happen. What you have in your head isn't going to be that reality, it's going to be just the opposite. "Nah sane, but check it out," (me imitating him) the homie was stubborn, his reality wasn't reality. He was stuck on what he was stuck on. I told him though, his way of thinking was the wrong type of thinking and his feelings were going to be hurt. Good homie though, good heart...but no bueno! Those are simply the wrong kind of thoughts to be having trying to get back out there after being gone so long, thinking you're going run something or have some type of say so! (SMH) Love you but nah! It's just not going to happen Big Bro. Many homies before him with that same attitude and thought process found out the hard way, leaving many niggahs whupped out or bagged. He was stuck on that, "Yeah, Sane...I'm just gon do this and do that!" (SMH) Those thoughts would fuck around and be a niggah's downfall. Dudes aren't playing fair, that's all I'm saying.

If he was really paying attention to what was going on, it had already taken place and was taking place presently and around him. Here it is we're locked up and doing what it is we do on the yard and mind you the G homie has been gone a long ass time. Don't get me wrong, when the G homie was younger he was gang gang and a beast, turned up (active and aggressive) and didn't give a fuck about flighting the police. He was with all of the shit, the race riots, the melees, the squabbles, the whole nine. My niggah was with the festivities over the years though, he hadn't had a 115, been to SHU or sat in the sandbox in a gang of years. His thing started to be him just falling back but would speak on issues and situations with the City, but when it actually started to become about internal issues or situations, he was pretty much hands off. He'd rather orchestrate the play (a DP) and would send other homies who he felt hadn't got their feet wet.

Some homies took that personal b'cuz he would use, "I have Board coming up Sane, I'm trying to get up out of here!" This, that and the third, Board this, Board that! "I'm trying to kick back Sane!" A'ight, I get that, these young niggahs ain't feeling it though. All they're hearing and seeing is you steady hollering about Board, but you're steady speaking on shit, trying to send niggahs and trying to have an input about shit, but not wanting to get in the rotation, using your "G" card. Every time it's talk about a homie having to be DP'ed or he's voted off the island, you're not volunteering to participate and quick to throw up Board this, Board that. Young homies are looking at you funny and looking at you sideways. I saw it and heard it (SMH). The whole thing is, if you're not participating and trying to go home, go home. Stop speaking on shit or trying to have input on something, trying to direct traffic.

It was a few homies on the yard one day, we were clowning, as we do. One of the younger homies said to the G homie, "Cuz, when was the last time you had a 115 or been to a SHU?" Though it was all in fun and they were clowning, he took offense to it, as if his gangster was in question. At that point he could only speak on old shit, not present shit and he was in his feels, feeling some type of way. The younger homies started laughing, but you could clearly see they respected him, just not as an active G homie. Me personally, I could see if a situation or an issue came about, he would be tried. My observation is, young homies don't respect and aren't going to feel being told something by a homie that isn't active and in the trenches and haven't been in a cool minute. That's like a niggah listening to a niggah telling another niggah how to regulate a relationship with his bitch and he don't have one (SMH). Niggah, if you don't knock it the fuck off! How the hell you're going to tell a dude about a bitch, anything, when you don't have one? I know I'm not going to listen at you or nothing you're talking about.

    I've had young homies tell me, "Shit, cuz, I'm just not gon listen to a mutha fucka that ain't active and just trying to send a mutha fucka and with every excuse in the book not to go!" Couldn't help but feel and overstand him. I wasn't mad at him, not at all! But yeah, back to what I was telling the G homie Rocc Head: "Don't get out cuz, and be on no bullshit. Niggahs out there is playing ball and ain't playing no games. You will come up missing and that's on some real shit!" We'll see though. I hope the homie got out and saw the turf isn't nothing like it he thought it would be and switched gears b'cuz the turf isn't the turf, which I'm sure he recognoticed. Moving along and switching lanes. I've touched on it briefly, but what really kills me is how after a gang of years have passed, and shit start coming out about G homies you wouldn't have ever suspected. Some way way back in the day type shit (SMH). This G homie had done some telling on a homie! Whaaat! And still able to hang out and be around.

## FEELING SOME TYPE OF WAY—SODO AUSTIN

Other G homies know and knew back then about a niggah being a rat bastard! A dirty vermin! It went viral amongst them (G homies).

One thing I came to know and overstand when it comes to G homies, they know how to keep shit to themselves and in their collective circles until they feel some type of way about something, then a niggah's getting aired out! (Dirty little secret being exposed.) Shit I still hear amazes me. I'm like, whaaat! (SMH) Though knowing some of the shit you hear, you have to take with a grain of sand b'cuz of Autobotism and bullshit of how G homies will feel a certain type of way about another G homie and will just smut a G homie up. Just being on some Mickey shit, a dude can just not like you or feel you and smut you up. Who's going to question it and he has Autobots? You might be fucking with another G homie that a G homie isn't feeling and somehow you're caught up in that shit! (SMH) Oh yeah, they do manipulate, they do hate, they do work out them fucked up kits, they are Mickey. They do snitch, they have snitched. A lot of their actions should be questioned, especially if they're doing suspect shit or have done suspect shit. Something to be mindful of, every G homie isn't a G homie and don't have a homie's or the turf's best interest at heart. Every homie who claims that G homie status isn't a G homie and doesn't have that status. The generation doesn't mean shit. Just b'cuz you're in a certain age group or from a certain era, it doesn't automatically make you a G homie, that's out! You just don't get that title if you haven't earned that title...East Side!

## FEELING SOME TYPE OF WAY—SODO AUSTIN

I'm quite sure the homies that are G homies from your age group or era will have something to say about it. You don't just get that based on. That's not how that works at all! I'm just saying. You don't get shit you don't deserve or have put in work for. Homies are going to makes sure of it. Going to let you know to stay in your lane Turbo, and in front of whoever. That's when young homies are going to see, too, a niggah isn't who he claims to be or acted to be, which is a G homie, see how he's "getting got at" (talked to), which is disrespectfully. It will have you looking at him instantly in a different light. I've seen that look too on the block (SMH), like, "Damn, I thought he was one of those ones (gang gang)." Come to find out he wasn't one of them ones (well respected G homie), far from it. Had a dude fooled like a mutha fucka. Talking that talk, walking that walk. Until he was exposed for who he really was and what he was really about. That image wasn't him.

It fucked me up to find out he was basically a bitch and he wasn't respected by other reputable G homies. I really had to evaluate my character judgment b'cuz dudes aren't who they pretend to be half of the time. They'll be who they want to be, wish to be, or allowed to be (SMH) until their cover's pulled and it's like, "Oh, that's who you are!" Seeing a dude for who he really is, seeing him for what he's really about. Dude was playing dress up, playing a part all along and was able to get away with it. Fooling dudes, especially younger homies coming up, have them thinking he's really truth and gang gang, when the reputable G homies are gone or have been wrapped up. Who's to refute it? He's flying under the radar. They don't know any better b'cuz he's all they know, thus he has their

## FEELING SOME TYPE OF WAY—SODO AUSTIN

support and energy, but not knowing it's under false pretenses though. Another thing too, young homies have to know and really really overstand, every G homie isn't going to have your best interest in mind or at heart.

And the relationship is basically on some fuck with you type shit b'cuz it fits his equation or narrative and it's in his best interest to do so. Fucking with you has to be beneficial. Anything less is a mis-overstanding. There's a big difference between fucking with you! And fucking with with you. They're not one in the same, there's always that difference. Fuck with you on some "part of" or "in their circle" type shit. That or it's fucking with you on some "see you and speak," basically acknowledge you type shit. They fuck with you but they don't fuck with you, confusing as it might be (SMH). Some you have to definitely watch b'cuz they're Mickey as a mutha fucka. Please believe it, especially if they have a "rep" for doing dirty shit to homies or having dirt done to homies, viral shit! The only time you don't have to worry about that type of G homie is if you're a part of that inner circle and on that same type of page. You know the saying, "Scandalous niggahs fuck with scandalous niggahs."

I overstand and came to overstand, some G homies get a bad rep too for doing shit they actually had nothing to do with. Didn't do it or wasn't a part of it. So they're easily branded and the fingers are pointed at them based on their rep and known for being Mickey with Mickey ways. Based on who they are, who they fuck with, who they're affiliated with. It had to be "him"/" them." And you know what? It's easy to just put it on "him"/" them." They stay getting blamed for shit, whether they had a hand or voice in it or not. Once you get that rep or label, it's a wrap. Dudes are always going to have you pegged, have that assumption of you and will always associate you with bullshit. Have to wear that. I personally know of a few G homies, but one in particular that according to most homies or homies you ask, he had that rep for doing dirt to homies and known for it.

    I can say too he gets blamed for a lot of shit that went on in the turf internally, even for shit for a fact he didn't do, but it's put on him, his crew and other homies he fucks with, when in fact a lot of the shit he gets blamed for or associated with wasn't him. But based on the rep, he got that. The cold thing about it though, ain't nobody going to tell him that to his face or pull up on him about anything! Let alone ask him if he done something or if he knows about this, that or the third. That isn't going to happen, and I can bang that! I've only had one minor situation with him and had to nip that in the bud. You can't have anything lingering in the air fucking wit him. You have to address it. He's definitely a shadow niggah. What might be a misdemeanor to you might be a felony to him. He'll take it somewhere else completely, never know wit him.

    We addressed it and left it at that, a misoverstanding. It appeared to be left alone, but keeping it one hunnid, I never fully trusted him or his word and always kept eyes on him and never turned my back on him. Put it like this, I would've went into no dark alley or space to talk to him about a mutha fucking thing! We're good in the open and in the light. I need to be able to see your hands, your eyes and feet I'm not worried about. I'm sure a whole lot of homies wouldn't of either. They can talk that shit like they would, but tell that bullshit to somebody that doesn't know any better that's shit you do! I'm not going for it b'cuz you're horseplaying! I know it and you know it! Yeah, I can bang that! B'cuz I ain't him and that ain't me! I fuck with my G homies and made it a point to fuck with them, even the ones that puffed (smoked dope) too and wasn't on the Mickey shit. It's quite a few of them too.

Yeah, yeah, yeah, boy do I have a few G homies puffing on that shit like broke stoves. It is what it is, though, still my homies. It doesn't take nothing from their gangster or their get down. They're still functional, still gang gang, that's just their drug choice. Some tried to shake it, but you know how that goes. For young homies, though, they stay having something to say about a G homie smoking. Stay with the jokey jokes, stay shooting them. Some of them try to get on some disrespectful shit, finding themselves getting punched on, choked out or whupped out! G homies be like, "Don't get it fucked up, lil niggah. I might smoke, but I'll still fuck your young ass up. You got me fucked up!" I saw that episode go bad a few times. Young homies getting a G homie confused b'cuz they're smoking and feel like they can just say what they want to or how they want to, being reckless with their tongue.

Feeling like you can just get at G homie sideways and he wasn't having it. It was no bueno! Ask a lot of homies that thought that and ask them how did that work out for them (SMH). I still trip off of some G homies, though, the ones on that shit (dope) and aren't functioning like that. You'll see them in the turf, but they're always on rock missions and

## FEELING SOME TYPE OF WAY—SODO AUSTIN

staying in the same dusty ass Pendleton, dusty ass beanie cap, ran down ass kicks and dusty ass pants. Which they've had on for days, smelling like ass, feet and stale ass smoke. You're like, "Damn, cuz, back your ass up off me, witchah stanking ass!" (SMH) and stay trying to fast talk you or swindle you, trying to come up on a hit or something. Oh, don't be a buster, you're about to be a victim. Definitely about to run your pockets or strip you out. These are the same G homies too that when you run across them in the County or in the "maze" they're gang gang and "turnt up" and big with the politics. Running the yard and have the keys for the homies. You'll be like whoa! Hold the fuck up. This is the same niggah on the streets smoked out, dusty, and niggahs wasn't really fucking with him (SMH).

That's what it is though. They're being all they can be, locked up. They know on the streets it's a whole different ballgame. Their push was way way different than what they're showing. Dudes on the outside looking in are seeing an illusion. On the streets it's, "Fuck all that, a niggah trying to get his Puff the Magic Dragon on." It doesn't affect all the G homies the same b'cuz it's that side of G homies smoking where that shit took their heart and their being gang gang, having homies from every generation fucking over them, treating them bad, talking crazy to them or just bullshit to them, based on. Some homies feel them, some don't, regardless of the fact though, they're not looked at the same, somebody feeling some type of way. They're going to be looked down on, based on, b'cuz they're off (on) the rocks. I sat back too and tripped off G homies that I know from the streets and have been around in the maze, seeing how

## FEELING SOME TYPE OF WAY—SODO AUSTIN

turnt up they get and are. I'm talking about big pushing. Homie straight reinvented himself. You're like again whoa! What's that about? (SMH).

You can't help but to be like, damn for real? Where's this fire and push on the streets? It fucks you up seeing this look, knowing what you know and how you know it. I don't buss dudes' bubbles though, or rain on their parades or piss in their corn flakes. You don't see the push or this fire, then when you do it's like kind of hard for some homies to accept. They're like, "Niggah, if you don't knock it off, this wasn't you on the streets in the turf, all of a sudden you're Mr. Politician and acting like you're somebody." Especially young homies, they're looking at a niggah on some "Niggah, you're a smoker on the streets" type shit. "You're not nobody, niggahs ain't fucking with you like that." I don't know what be going through their minds.

I guess they feel being locked up they can be all they can be, big line pusher, big politician! "G homie." Their weight's up, they're working out and their feeling themselves. It's like they've reinvented themselves. That only lasts while their wrapped up. As soon as they're back in the turf, after a few weeks it's the same ole three step niggah back puffing. Then you see them and it's like, "What's good, cuzzo?" He's like, "Shit, a niggah's out here getting my hustle on!" (SMH) Still wearing his parole clothes, looking like he's been up for a week. You're looking him up and down like, "Yeah, niggah, what the fuck ever...out here getting my hustle on!" You're getting your hustle on all right. Dude's back dusty, back stinking, but this time he went from smelling like ass, feet and stale smoke to ass, feet and train smoke.

You can clearly see dude hasn't changed his clothes in at least a week and can smell him a mile away. There's a lot of homies like him running around and from a lot of turfs. We all have those types of G homies. You'll hear a lot of, "Look at this smokin ass niggah...here comes this smokin ass mutha fucka!" Not respecting the homie or his get down. A lot of times he's disregarded, dismissed and some more shit. To some, the niggah's in the way, he's only trying to be a somebody b'cuz he's wrapped up. The only dudes taking him serious in the maze or jail period are young homies that don't know better. Once they figure him out though, it's a wrap, they aren't going to look at him the same, respond to him the same or fuck with him the same. But yeah, to the G homies that's gang gang, still pushing, in and out of the maze, still in the mix, I tip my hat to you. Only the ones that are keeping it a hunnid, aren't with the Mickey shit or dirty politics, I fucks with you.

Niggahs can count on you to keep it hard it in the paint and to speak your mind. Even when it comes to other G homies that aren't playing fair, hands down. Yet dudes don't get and can't overstand why young homies don't have that same love and respect they do for other G's, wondering why it is they can't make a call and have it respected. Wondering why it is young homies fuck with you the way that they do. It's b'cuz you're the opposite of the homie that does get and overstand why young homies have that love and respect for them. They don't have to

## FEELING SOME TYPE OF WAY—SODO AUSTIN

worry about making a call and having it not respected. They don't have to worry about a young homie not moving. They already know why it is young homies fuck with them the way that they do and like being around them. Their get down is transparent, how they get down all the way around the board is A-1. Their 360 is done how it's supposed to be done period, point blank.

There's nothing flawed or faulty about their gang gang, they're solid and looked at in high regard. The respect and loyalty didn't come from scare tactics or intimidation, dudes aren't fucking with you b'cuz they're afraid of you. A dude can't do nothing but respect it! ...East Side! For the G homies that are on the Mickey shit and with the Mickey shit, y'all need to knock it off! ...East Side!

# Chapter 10

## "It Get Real"

It gets real as fuck, fucking around with this lifestyle as it is and as it really is and for what it really is. Peeling back all of the different layers of the bullshit and getting past all of the illusions of truth, being hidden behind the mask of deception. This lifestyle isn't for the faintest of hearts and as I've said always, gang banging or being in the streets aren't for everyone. Every dude isn't built for this shit. Like the streets aren't made for every dude and why banging isn't for every dude. The lifestyle that we live as bangers and street niggahs is cold as fuck. The experiences and exposures we're subjected to and subject ourselves to. This shit is far from being a joke and should never be taken for granted. We're constantly experiencing all praise is due to Allah and to Allah we belong and to Him we return moments. We experience loss, disappointment, frustrations, Autobotism, Gilliganism, hate, hatred, love, death, fear, lies, amongst a lot of other shit. We come to realize shit that we wouldn't have ever expected from so-called friends and homies, surprisingly enemigos too. (SMH) Enemigos or a dude, peers in general.

Coming to realize just how this shit gets and can get bluey bluey! Some come to realize this sooner than others and know how to get the fuck out of the way. Being on some "fuck it" type shit, being "cool on it" (leaving it alone), like this isn't for the kid and do it moving. Off the dribble recognoticing what it is, seeing what it is or what it can be and rather not indulge period. Recognoticing the streets aren't made for

## FEELING SOME TYPE OF WAY—SODO AUSTIN

everyone, as banging isn't. It's no bueno! It doesn't take much nowadays to turn a dude off, especially nowadays with how the state of the game is, it's watered down! In all essence, it's garbage and it's Mickey. That's just keeping it a hunnid with you. First and foremost though, the snitching is just off the hinges, out of control and to damn it all, it's just the norm now (SMH). Dudes are weaponizing it and using it as a form of warfare, especially enemigos, they take the case.

They'll actually come to court on you and get on the stand, pointing directly the fuck at you while testifying against you. "Him right there, he shot the homie, or he done this, that and the third!" You'll be looking at this rat bastard like what the fuck! (SMH) While their homies are in the courtroom for moral and homie support, trying to look hard (SMH). That's just crazy, actually in the courthouse trying to look hard and act hard, but in the same breath support a mutha fucka snitching! (SMH) How in the fuck does that work though? How does that work? Riddle me that, cuz! Your homie up in there telling on a mutha fucka and you and your homies are up in there listening to this shit, seeing this shit. It's like wow...really? What part of the game and get down is that? That shit is way out! They're straight condoning switchism and supporting it (SMH) now with dudes doing it internally it's even more way out and off the hinges. B'cuz it's always the one you least expect it to be. I can bang that too! Then it's that element of a niggah you think is a homie finds himself getting wrapped up in a Mickey situation unrelated and doesn't have shit to do with you, but all of a sudden he makes his situation your situation.

## FEELING SOME TYPE OF WAY—SODO AUSTIN

Now you're wrapped up b'cuz he used your situation that he knew about against you to get a get out off jail free card (SMH) Rat bastard! His whole mindset, mind frame, was basically fuck it! "I know something I can use to get me out of my situation, I'm going to shoot my shot!" He does just that! (SMH) Fuck what the repercussions are, not realizing just how bad it's about to go for him. He crossed a line he can't cross back over.

He let "pressured up" put him into a situation. Cold thing about it, it's done more than you would think too. That's going on everywhere, your turf, my turf and the next dude's turf (SMH). A dude can know something or has dirt on you and instead of sweeping it under the rug, forgetting about it, to him it can be used as leverage and as a means to get up out of some shit if need be. If it just so happens to fit the equation and narrative, it is what it is. I seen it too many times, fucking with dudes nowadays, you have to be mindful of dudes and mindful of dudes surrounding you. It isn't all what it seems. That's me being Bitterchild advocate too, straight up, straight down. Back in the day, in my earlier years getting off the porch, a niggah done a whole lot of shit I'd gotten away with as a banger and as a young niggah in the streets of Long Beach, on the East Side. Slanging work and jacking. I came to overstand a lot and came to separate the differences between what was and what wasn't.

I also had come to have a greater respect for certain shit, due to what came with it or behind it, at the end of the day. Everything else, I shot my shot on some street niggah shit...stand up type. always took my

## FEELING SOME TYPE OF WAY—SODO AUSTIN

lumps and bruises, keeping the line moving, knowing what I signed up for. As for what I didn't sign up for, it's just a part of it. A dude can be a real niggah or a bitch made niggah, forget about what the next dude's doing or isn't doing or how he's getting down. That's what's wrong with dudes nowadays, worrying too much about the wrong thing. Do you! It's homies that know a lot of it and was around for a lot of it back then. Then some are resting in peace now, have passed on since I've been wrapped up, as far as homies knowing my dirt and how I was doing me (banging, jacking, etc.). For those though, that still exist and are around, I don't worry about them b'cuz if they were going to expose my dirt, my shit would've been exposed years ago.

So that just shows you the type of dudes I messed with and was around, real to the grave with it type niggahs and visa versa. But nowadays I would be worried about my skeletons and bones buried, knowing a mutha fucka knew anything about them (SMH). Dudes are doing gang drugs, drinking, blowing trees and talking too fucking much. They're even spooning and pillow talking with these whore bags they're in situationships with. (SMH) Just talking to make themselves seem more important or bigger than they are...bigger than they really are. Nowadays I would be worried about a mutha fucka knowing something, b'cuz you'll never know when a mutha fucka will up and just decide to put you out there, airing you out, b'cuz they were wrapped up their out is to use what they know about you. That's too much to be on a niggah's mind, worrying and wondering about every time a niggah that knows something gets wrapped up, is he going to air you out b'cuz he's on some bitch niggah shit (SMH).

Oh yeah, it gets real in the field...suuuper! Dudes are spooked to do shit and have homies know about it, you'll find yourself told on. Every dude ain't to be trusted, homie or not, and every dude isn't meant to be trusted. It's a reason for that, I've shared many with you. This shit ain't a joke, homie, it's real in the field, I'm telling you, and gets much realer. It's not even a good look doing something and then going through the turf telling homies, it's not safe being on the block or in the turf. You're basically pulling up, letting dudes know you just put in some work on enemigo and to get the fuck off of the streets just in case they decide to pull back up on some "get back" (retaliation). But here it is, you're not trying to leave them in the dark on the "get down," on some do the right thing type shit. Trying to look out, not being on no selfish shit, out of concern for their wellbeing and safety.

It's suuuper easy not to say nothing and be on some "fuck niggahs," on some self-preservation shit, letting the chips fall where they may. It isn't like homies would've known. That it was you who pulled up on enemigo and "got off" (shot at them), having them pull up afterwards. That would be between you, Allah and whoever it was you put in work on if it wasn't a solo type deal. Your thing though, being a real homie keeping it real, you want to give the homies a heads up so they're just not out all willy-nilly. Out willy-nilly being targets if enemigo decide to pull up and holler back. Your just looking out, you're not thinking a mutha fucka in the crowd or on the block is going to use it against you, on the thirty-third (a later time).

Cold thing though, it is going to be one and it's going to be one that's going to use it if he has to. Whether it's a dude you fuck with on a daily or not, being pressured up, buss pipes, blooommm! Truth of the matter is that's just what's going to happen, it's been locked in a dude's mind for a later time (SMH). A few homies had that very shit done to them, fresh off putting in work on enemigo, running through on their way to switch swoops, hollering out, "Aye, we just served some Baldheads on the West Side and laid they ass out, don't be out, get off the streets." Just like that, on the thirty-third it came back to bite them in their ass, on the left cheek too. One of the homies went to the maze with 15 or 18 years, the other one 22 or 23 (SMH). Something like that, mind you though, the homie with the most time ended up tapping out, taking his batteries out behind some bullshit he got caught up in, in the maze, then went home and got took down by fentanyl (SMH).

Another homie was voted off the island behind leaving homies in the dark. That's when keeping it to the chest went wrong. The mind state being, "Shit, I'm not about to tell a niggah a God damn thing. Why? So they can run and tell on me later? That's out! I'm not going to be able to do it, K.T.S.E.!" That's the mind state of dudes nowadays, though, regardless. They know the game that's being played and how dudes are pressing play and they're feeling some type of way. It's just crazy and burnt out how dudes are getting down and will get down. But that's what it is, dudes aren't playing fair! At all. You'll find out too how dudes you've been looking up to, been fucking with having respect for and major love for, aren't who you thought they were (SMH). Dudes are Mickey! Dudes are turning out to be snitches...raaats! (SMH) Suspects and weirdos! Reputable homies, G homies and big homies, it's like wow, for real?!

    It's going to have you looking at dudes and looking at situations in a whole different light or manner. Going to have you looking at things and seeing them for what they are and as they really are. All along dudes had dirt on their handle (name) and they were foul, turnt up niggahs too. It's going to fuck you up b'cuz you had an image of a dude and looked at him a certain type of way and what you came to know wasn't going to add up, it just wouldn't. Then you're going to be in denial on some, "Nah, not such and such, not my boy, that's not his demo. He's solid," type shit, or on some, "Not him, homie straight!" Come the thirty-third though, it's wow A niggah can't believe it, it's out of character. Then your mind is going to go on rewind mode and keying in on all the little shit you overlooked, and the shit you recognoticed that was and has always been suspect to you. Dude's certain movements, certain dudes being fucked with, certain niggahs being fucked with, niggahs aren't fucking with them...no bueno!

    You're going to play back all types of shit and scenarios, trying to make it make sense, b'cuz it's just hard to accept this niggah's foul or suspect. I've gotten a bar of that look on more than one occasion, hearing about this G homie or that G homie, hearing about this big homie or that big homie, hearing about this BG or that BG, this young or that baby (SMH) being on some foul shit or went bad (snitched, was voted off the

## FEELING SOME TYPE OF WAY—SODO AUSTIN

island, or took his batteries out). A niggah done went bad, done some telling on a homie back in the day. Been went bad though, it was just kept on the hush hush (SMH), on like some "circle" or "crew" lil dirty secret type shit. Certain homies being privy to the get down. It just makes you think, what else niggah's know and aren't speaking on about homies. "Every" and I do mean "every" turf has "dirty lil secrets" that only a few know about. Over the years though, they'll surface behind someone working with F and E's, and feeling some type of way.

    Feeling some type of way about a certain situation or incident and it's aired out. I've seen it to the point of witnessing a homie say some shit to another homie like, "Niggah, you suspect anyway. How only one niggah go to jail, but two niggahs jacked a mutha fucka, got caught, caught with bangers and on parole?" Whaaat! The dude laughed it off, saying, "Fuck you, niggah!" and just changed the subject. Hold up, flag on the play! This niggah just called you a snitch. You ain't feeling some type of way? Or working with no type of F and E's? That's all you have is a laugh, and a weak laugh at that, and fuck you niggah? (SMH) What part of the script is that though? He was just nonchalant about it and wasn't feeling no type of way, no type at all.

    It's a lot of shit that goes on, though, then when you "get a bar" (gain knowledge), it's going to have you rethinking your position about how you fuck with homies and rightfully so. Shit isn't all what it appears to be or what it's cracked up to be, too much bullshit being put in the game, then add the gang drugs, cold mixture I can bang that too! ...East

## FEELING SOME TYPE OF WAY—SODO AUSTIN

Side! This shit is suuuper watered down. How can you respect it when it's not being respected? Niggahs are turncoats, will turn on you, will switch up on you quick as fuck, if it's going to fit some narrative or equation. They're going to go with what's going to benefit them the most and benefit their agenda. Fuck what y'all have going on or how y'all fucked with each other. They're going to fuck with these other dudes, b'cuz they feel they can further their cause a lot quicker than fucking with you.

Certain homies come around, they're trying to get in with, they'll be on some suuuper funny shit with you. Dudes start clowning and bagging (joking) with them, but they're on you. That part of it isn't shit, it just shows though, how quick a dude will jump sides on you. That's my whole thing, the turncoat shit on some trivial shit or not. It shows a dude's character. I recognotice all that type of shit and put it in my mental Rolodex, especially if it comes just so easy to a mutha fucka to do. If you're a turncoat, it just says you're not a loyal dude b'cuz you'll turn on a dude and don't have a problem with doing it, it can be some political shit too. Instead of going with what's right or what's real, your character says you'll go with what the majority's pushing at that moment, taking an Autobot position. Who's to say, someone doesn't have a hidden agenda and pushing dirty politics, though, playing dirty ball? Which dudes are known for doing and having done. It's gotten dudes voted off the mutha fuckin island, kick rocks, get up outtah here! It got dudes bagged and banged.

Dirty politics is basically getting dudes to side with you on some manufactured shit or some foul shit, against the next niggah b'cuz you're

## FEELING SOME TYPE OF WAY—SODO AUSTIN

feeling some type of way about a situation or feel threatened by a niggah. Dirty politics are easy to press play on, so it's a go to. It can even be b'cuz you're feeling he's more gang gang than you and has the rep you feel you're supposed to have, b'cuz you've been from the turf longer, but he's outshining you...suuuper! You're not feeling that! It can really be b'cuz you know he has some dirt on you that you don't want to come out, so you're campaigning to turn dudes against him to discredit him if he does decide to air you out, on that indiscretion. Whatever it was...on some "beatchah to the punch" type shit. So at every little turn, you're bad mouthing or speaking on a niggah, saying shit like, "This niggah's suspect, this niggah did or said this, that and the third." All types of bullshit to plant seeds in dudes' minds to turn them against dude. (SMH)

He'll even go so far as saying, "I think such and such said this niggah spoke on how he had something to do with such and such getting bagged!" On the streets or in the maze. If it's in the maze, it'll get as dirty as dirty ass paperwork being manufactured and produced, saying you told on some shit that happened...niggahs horseplaying (SMH). It isn't an end a niggah won't go to or get to, to get dudes to turn on you, being on some bullshit and orchestrating the bullshit, if that's the agenda (SMH). His objective is to get you DP'ed or voted off the island, all b'cuz he's feeling some type of way about you. So he has to shift the attention your way before it gets to him, blowing his ass up out of the water. For no other reason than you might have some dirt on him (SMH).

You might have more status than he does (SMH). It doesn't even have to be an issue with a certain dude, a dude will politic you on some

## FEELING SOME TYPE OF WAY—SODO AUSTIN

dirty shit b'cuz a dude he fuck with don't like you. The dirty politics can come about in "a gang" (a lot) of different ways. A dude can be getting his rabbs and b'cuz dudes feel he's not sharing the wealth or breaking bread, here comes the shenanigans, the Mickey shit and being "bumped up" (asked questions)(SMH). "This niggah's not doing this, that and the third." "This niggah ain't letting homies eat." "This niggah ain't putting nothing in the turf." "Homies can't get no bangers." The next thing you know, "He's really not from the turf like that anyway, that niggah don't even be in the turf really, half the time the niggah just pushing through throwing up the turf, doing no stopping, fuckin with no homie." "He ain't put in no work, who can vouch for the niggah putting in work?"

After that, it's fuck that niggah, we're going to do this, that and the third to him. Dudes are riled up and ready to trip on a niggah. Then he's going to find himself tripped on and jacked on more than one occasion, until he's pressured up to do something. But for no other reason though, than he's getting rabbs, doing him (living his life). He's not doing anything the next dude isn't doing or can't do. But you know what I've come to realize, niggahs are going to always find a reason to trip on a mutha fucka. It's just niggahs for you, being niggahs! It is what it is. They'd rather see you down than up, it's just a known fact. At the end of the day, you have to know, have to know and overstand the different elements that come with banging and being in the streets.

It's real cruel, it's cold, it's calculating, it's manipulating, it's imminent death, it's imminent jail, it's constantly having to admit and

## FEELING SOME TYPE OF WAY—SODO AUSTIN

trying to get your mind around shit. It's illusions of truth wearing masks of deception well and it's loss. You're going to find yourself doing a whole lot of drinking, a whole lot of gang drugs, a whole lot of sherm and tree blowing, to the point of trying to numb yourself. At some point, though it starts to become too much and it starts fucking with a dude, so you turn up the drinking, the gang drugs, the sherm and the trees (SMH). The shit niggahs see, the shit they do, the shit they're around, the shit they know. So they stay looking for coping mechanisms, not to mention deal with situationships and baby mama drama (SMH). But yeah, some just take their batteries out and be like fuck it, "I'm straight, I'm not built for this shit."

    I can respect that dude, though. He had the sense to recognotice how he was and wasn't built. He didn't want to play with the game, seeing firsthand how well that works out for a mutha fucka. It doesn't pay nowadays to get into it with certain homies, b'cuz if it goes there you might as well whip out (draw your weapon) and get off on him. He'll be looking to get at you first chance he gets, on the thirty third, feeling some type of way. B'cuz y'all might've squabbled up (fought) and you got the best of him from the shoulder, he suuuper wasn't feeling that "L" (loss), damn sure wasn't accepting it (SMH). Y'all might've had words, wasn't feeling that either, like he can't be gotten at verbally a certain type of way. He's on some, "Yeah, let me catch you slipping in the wee wee hours in the turf, I'm a blow your beans (brains) out." It's a lot of his type in the hood, yours, mine and the next niggah's, it's viral.

## FEELING SOME TYPE OF WAY—SODO AUSTIN

When you find homies bagged in the turf, it's not enemigo's doing it a lot of the time, but it's the first thing a mutha fucka will assume or say it was enemigo who got the homie. In reality though, it was a homie who got the homie...whaaat? (SMH) And more than likely behind some bullshit. Some bullshit that didn't warrant a niggah getting bagged. A dude fucking with a bitch? Come on, homie, she's everybody's bitch. What niggah's not fucking on the bitch? It's not like a dude doesn't know she's fucking out of both pant legs, she's a turf rat. She's straight up a whore bag. A niggah got out faded (beat up) from the shoulders, damn for real? You can't whup a niggah, fuck it, huh? Just bag the homie! (SMH) The homie got at you like you were trying to get at him and you didn't like that, so it's fuck this niggah, I'm going to bag him. Then the damn it all, you're popping up at the funeral with the "tee" on, with the homie's captured moment and the rest in peace on it, along with everyone else and the homies (SMH). Cold ass niggah, huh? But we know that goes on.

It goes to show you though, a dude's mind state, but it's a dude we all know too well. You have to always keep your eye on this dude, both eyes. Can't get laxed around this type of dude, either. He's always on some Mickey shit and with no good reason, just b'cuz. As it always happens though, this niggah himself ends up getting bagged b'cuz homies deem you a "wild dog" and bag you! Proven fact, dogs that are wild get euthanized, quick, fast and in a hurry. Homies will play ball on you. So watch it, with your shenanigans! Or you're up out of here. Who's going to really give a fuck about you getting bagged? You're the same niggah in the turf on the Mickey shit! Shit, dudes were done a favor getting rid of you. But that's how the shit happens. Every one of them type of dudes don't get to keep existing. It's always a matter of time before it's an all praise is due to Allah, to Allah we belong and to Him we return moment.

    Being on and with the shit they're on and be on, without a doubt your days are numbered. A dude will find himself getting done, how he'd been doing dudes, that boomerang effect and I can bang that. No longer fitting dude's equations, so you had to go. Once any dude isn't fitting the equation no longer, it's basically a wrap. You're pretty much expendable, my niggah, homie to homie. That homie shit doesn't matter, not at all. Homies will serve you and wouldn't think twice about it. Will start plotting your exit and will be fucking wit you on a daily as if shit's all gravity, then you're up out of here. On some suuuper real niggah shit, don't get to doing too much and homies start feeling like you're doing too much, b'cuz it's a bad look and you're not being felt, that can't go no way but bad! Its imminent once homies are feeling some type of way. At that point you're already politiced on and voted off the island, only you're not knowing.

    Arrogant and cocky niggahs set themselves up for failure every time, as if they're untouchable or un-fadable. (SMH) Can't be on no cocky or arrogant shit. Like with bullies, cockiness and arrogance finds you caught the fuck up, on some false sense of security type shit, due to their belief they're bigger than what they think, or they're above something. I'm here to say, it's no bueno! You aren't...proven fact! Reality checks aren't no joke, reality checks get just as real. You'll learn what it is quick, fast and in a hurry. You'll learn at the end of the day, the streets don't give a fuck about you. A niggah don't give a fuck about you and a bitch sure don't give

## FEELING SOME TYPE OF WAY—SODO AUSTIN

a fuck about you. You'll learn how easy your ass can be had and become a victim, how easy it is to have you and have at you.

Do overstand, when it gets real and gets real, and can go zero to sixty in a heartbeat. Shit can blow up on you, blooom! And you can't do a mutha fucking thing about it to stop it. Can't stop what you don't know or aren't privy to. It's going to take its course and play out how it's going to play out. Sometimes shit is just unavoidable and is imminent, can't be gotten around, it's out of your hands or control, it's in the stars. it'll be a lot of those moments, as with your being vulnerable. Vulnerability is just a reality, the hardest of the hardest be subjected to vulnerabilities. It doesn't make you soft or make you a buster b'cuz of your vulnerability. It makes you real, it has you recognoticing real. The realness of it for what it is, as it is.

It gets real when a mutha fucka gets bagged or gets banged. It gets real when a mutha fucka gets bussed on or gets aired out. It gets real when a mutha fucka gets whupped out, packed out or gets snitched on by a so-called homie! It really gets real when you find out you're not the mutha fucka you thought you were. You know when else it gets real though, when a mutha fucka's in a shootout and you run out of shells or your banger jams on you...not a good look. Most definitely not a good feel. A dude's heart rate is up and your mind's running full throttle and a thousand miles a minute. All types of shit is running through your mind, scenarios and outcomes. I know how those emotions work and look, felt and looked like when I was in an alley being "bussed" (shot) at and I didn't have a

## FEELING SOME TYPE OF WAY—SODO AUSTIN

banger and couldn't buss back (SMH). I just had to wait a mutha fucka out and hoped like a mutha fucka he didn't come up the alley where a niggah was, tucked between a gate and a telephone pole. (SMH)

    Fucked up feeling, waiting for a mutha fucka to come get you. I can only imagine how a homie felt when he was getting chased by enemigo and hopped in a trashcan in an alley waiting to be got at. Oh yeah, it got real for the homie, really real (I.I.P.). It gets real when G homies throw a meeting at a secret location in the city with a few younger homies, BG's and "Youngs" who were supposed to show up mando and were told not to bring no type of banger whatsoever. Basically wanting the young homies, BG's and Youngs to come unarmed. So they'll be the only ones armed. Me being one (a BG), I know I felt uncomfortable based on a few G homies that I knew who would be present and knew would be heated, based on their being gang gang and b'cuz of their reps. So a few of us went against the grain anyway and brought bangers on some "you never know" type shit.

    You never know how shit's going to transpire or play out, especially with all parties concerned and present. As far as those G homies, and that's just keeping it a hunnid with you suuuper! They can get on some Mickey shit and it's going crooked quick, fast and in a hurry, I can bang that! Especially with active G homies. You know when else it gets real? When a niggah you fuck with on a daily turn on you and will be the first to bag you, bang you, hate on you, or snitch on you (SMH). Same niggah you grew up with, same niggah you played in the mud with, ate mud pies with, will be the same niggah who will plot on you with the next homie and will vote you off the island. It get and also gets real when you're talking shit to a homie, as if you don't know he's gang gang and turnt the fuck up!

Finding yourself bussed in the mouth, fired on or whupped out. How again, when you beat a niggah's ass and he comes back heated (armed) and buss on you (SMH). It's your as, though, Mr. Postman. Dudes aren't accepting no ass whuppin's, let's get that clear though. They aren't about the hands and will feel pressured up b'cuz that's not what they really do. They're really not about none of that, unless they just have to be. If they just had to be, it is what it is, niggahs just have to shoot their shot. At the end of the day though, it's not about throwing your hands up, whether you're on the streets or in the maze. Dude's aren't doing no squabbling nowadays. They're whipping out on you, especially a young niggah, suuuper! They're getting off. On the streets, they'd just rather spark your ass up! Yup, can bang that too! On some real shit, you can't be running around putting your hands on mutha fuckas, just can't do it and I wouldn't advise it. Dudes are playing ball, ain't having it.

You will fuck around and get bagged, most definitely get banged. Dudes are just quick, too quick to pull that trigger. Most dudes nowadays coming up don't have a squabble game, so it's their only option to take it to the next page. Dudes aren't playing no type of games. Had a homie, a young homie who was bagged as he slept on the couch with a bitch on the couch with him, behind some shit like that. Not by a homie from the turf directly but by a homie allowing it to happen by his action. It gets real and

## FEELING SOME TYPE OF WAY—SODO AUSTIN

is real when you don't respect the politics of the streets, of the turf or the maze. As with anything, though, you don't respect it, it's going to be a bad look and your bad. I want my words to resonate with you and not being taken with a grain of sand.

This shit is real life. Well, I guess on that note I'll yet again park my pen to conclude this chapter of mine, as it is with and by me. I hope though, the impression I'm leaving will be a lasting one and locked into your mental Rolodex. If nothing else, having my words resonate with you, for that's my intent and my only intent as I've kept the content as real as real is and without diluting it. To tell you what I've told you and said in the manner it was expressed, it was me telling you my exposures and experiences as they were with me and others. To have told you though, I had to tell you theirs as only I did and could, without compromising anything or anyone, especially the integrity of what was being said, to paint that bigger captured moment. A'ight, remember and overstand, it gets real...and it gets realer!

# Chapter 11

"Loyalty"

Standing by someone through thick and thin and against all odds, win, lose or draw. You're fucking with them, you're ducking with them, straight up! Loyalty...it used to mean something to dudes and actually carried weight with them, held value. You had dudes actually loyal, standing by it, sticking to the script. Shocking, huh? I know (SMH). Nowadays, dude's loyalty can be bought and sold for a little of nothing. Loyalty today isn't the same loyalty I knew. Today's loyalty you have to question it b'cuz of the breed of dudes and how they've been taught, who they've been taught by (SMH). If all you're seeing are un-loyal dudes and un-loyal activities, more than likely it's going to be easy to conform or adapt, especially if it's seen by dudes admiring dudes that are gang gang and reputable. Dudes nowadays can't grasp that concept no more, or they do but the attitude is fuck it! I'm going to sag it out (SMH). "The next niggah ain't loyal, so why should I be loyal to a niggah?" I mean, that's dudes' mindset. I see what loyalty is, fucking with these Gilligans and Autobots and the dudes they are following.

    Will straight turn on you, turn their back on you, cross you like an intersection, will fuck up in your bitch if she opens her legs or her cheeks. The shit is Mickey. Dudes' loyalties are suspect and They're off of the radar. You'll never know just how loyal a niggah is or a bitch for that matter until their loyalty is tested though, and they have to expose themselves. But yeah, dudes act like this shit is a foreign concept or hard to do. It's not a foreign concept nor is it hard. Being loyal is the easiest thing in the world to be, easy as fuck. Loyalty is keeping it real, being real. It's keeping it all the way clean and is one hunnid with someone you have love for, with a genuine respect. It's having their back regardless and being counted on and counted for, to a fault. It's not going to waver nor be faulty and can stand any storm presented in the streets or the maze, both being unbalanced.

Loyalty is what a dude values most and can value most. What is a relationship or a connection without loyalty? This is someone you're supposed to feel, are bound with and fuck with on a daily and are down with, your boy. Especially if you feel they're your niggah, your road dog, your ace, your homie. They're for you, you're for them, they're there for you, you're there for them regardless. "When you need me, call." You're with them against all odds and can for sure be counted on when you're called on. "You pull up!" It's like, "What's the deal, homie? What are we on?" "What, you need rabbs? I got you!"

Loyalty is handling "wax" (business) that needs to be handled for your boy, if for some reason he's unable to. He should be able to rely and depend on you, as you should be able to depend and rely on him. Does it mean lie for them if it came to it? No doubt though, if it's going to get them out of a Mickey situation. Regardless of who has to be lied to to benefit the outcome, especially the "Ones." "Yeah, he was with me and we were chilling and watching the Colts and Raider game. He hadn't left." No matter how big or small a situation is, you're there. A dude's loyalty should

## FEELING SOME TYPE OF WAY—SODO AUSTIN

never have to be questioned. A dude's loyalty should always reflect you're loyal and you have your boy's back, point blank. Anything other than that is a misoverstanding and dude's loyalty needs to be questioned and he needs to be backed up on. If you can't be loyal or worthy of loyalty what type of niggah are you? You're basically working with a major character flaw, is all I can say.

Dudes just assume loyalty is automatic, that's no bueno! Loyalty doesn't come automatically, it's earned. If a dude's get down isn't right, he doesn't get that. You know what else loyalty is? Your boy knowing if you do a "lick" (robbery) and you get separated and you just so happen to get wrapped up by the "Ones," you're not saying shit and vice versa. It's gravity, no worries about your door being kicked in at two...three...in the morning, with banger pointing at you. "Don't move, mutha fucka!" (SMH) A dude isn't worried about that, none of that, that's the last shit a dude has to worry about. Don't have to worry about a niggah recording a statement in the substation. A niggah doesn't have surveillance on his ass and isn't folding or bending, being pressured up when pressure's applied, it's getting "sagged out" (dealing with the matter however!), you can pretty much count on that. You don't have to worry about the faulty shit or question a dude's get down, his loyal...is loyal. What a dude values most is a loyal friend and when you get one you keep them. Now though, as it is, you have to question the very essence of what loyalty is. Loyalty isn't part-time or comes with conditions and it's twenty-four seven, it's three hunnid and sixty-five days. Dudes have it and has it wrong. For some they have it twisted, it's not ever conditional, it's not ever watered down, it's never that thirty-third shit. For the most part, dudes have to know who the fuck they're dealing with.

Sometimes you won't know just how loyal a dude is or to what extent it is until your back is up against the wall and you're basically wrapped up, the shit's just out of control or to the point of having a dude pressured up. Then that's when the exposure comes into play and is visual. It's also exposed when a major issue pops up, there's no getting around it. You're going to see what you didn't get to see otherwise b'cuz it was disguised. There's nothing there to conceal it now, the disguise is over. What he's about is in the air, suuuper! Then its like, "Damn, I misjudged this niggah!" Yeah, you're feeling some type of way and rightfully so, b'cuz he was off the radar on you, having you think something that wasn't. You have dudes locked up with all day (life) and aren't coming home for a minute, but do have a lifeline with a lot of these bullshit ass laws they've come with being changed or amended. Or dudes having a gang of time and won't see the "bricks" (home) for a "good minute" (a long time) due to being stuck and all b'cuz of a rat bastard told on them.

Straight came to court, got on the stand and gave it up (SMH), telling everything they knew. Every and anything else they could think of to tell on a niggah to get them "booked" (convicted). Went big on the stand, the whole nine yards was pointing and all of that. (SMH) Supposed to be boys, homies (SMH). Thought they were loyal. Why wouldn't we believe it, being around these dudes and messing with them on a daily basis. In the streets with them, hustling with them, blowing with them, ducking with them, shooting or squabbling with them, like niggahs do. All along though, they're leading us to think otherwise by doing and saying all the right things. I mean, these are the dudes we're surrounding ourselves with and are surrounded by. Feeling they have our six, feeling they were real niggahs. As I've stressed, you're not going to know the extent of dudes' loyalty until a situation comes about and exposes (SMH).

Fake as fuck! Like with an instance I can think back on with a homie who had changed his name (turf name) to another homie's name that certain other homies didn't really "feel" (like) like that and felt some type of way about, feeling the homie wasn't being loyal for not sticking with the name of a homie he was representing from the turf (an older homie). When the homies heard he changed his name and to the name of a homie they weren't feeling, they weren't feeling it and were big in their feelings. I think the homie done it for the most part to part to piss niggahs off, b'cuz loyal he is. That I can attest to and he's gang gang! But shit, here it is the homie was fucking with homies that were considered public enemy #1. Mind you, a lot of homies weren't feeling these homies like that and felt some type of way about them due to most feeling like these homies were anti-homie if you weren't a part of them or what they were on. Mickey shit! These were the homies everyday niggahs on the streets, fucking with them, ducking with them. Some homies fucked with them but most didn't, couldn't trust them, not even a little bit, b'cuz of how the got down on homies (SMH). Keeping it a hunnid, I don't think no homie

## FEELING SOME TYPE OF WAY—SODO AUSTIN

trust them, even homies that do fuck with them. They're gang gang and they play ball, period.

They're known for politicing and for being the orchestrators of the bullshit, known for being turnt up, known for sagging it out, also known for getting at enemigos and on homies. So when the homie got wrapped up for his "hot topic" (murder) and got at these homies about tapping in with a homie that was telling, all they kept telling him was they were on it, but "on it" never came. So he felt betrayed and felt they weren't loyal or being loyal. Hell yeah, he was feeling some type of way about it. The homie was working with F and E's b'cuz after all they'd been through with each other and how they got down with each other, he felt they were family, but they could see him with that. So his attitude was fuck you niggahs then! Knowing though, that if the "Chuck" was on the other foot based on his loyalty to them, it would've been handled. The niggahs was dunzo! For sure he wasn't coming to court on a niggah...

Seeing they weren't as loyal to him as he thought, knowing how loyal he was to them and to the extent he was willing to go for any of them in his circle, it fucked him up. He couldn't get his mind around it, as far as he was concerned and seeing what he saw from niggahs he was loyal to, having major love and respect for, he was on some fuck you niggahs type shit. "I'm straight on you niggahs. I ain't fucking with you no more." And he backed up, cutting ties, thus changed his name...East Side! By him changing his name to a homie they weren't feeling, he was saying, "Fuck you," with a statement (his actions). But yeah, the homie got a real bar about loyalty and how fake niggahs push. How un-loyal niggahs push.

## FEELING SOME TYPE OF WAY—SODO AUSTIN

Saying and doing all the right things to have the homie feel like they had him and was for and about him, being a part of them and their circle. (SMH) Dudes are loyal to what they're loyal to and loyal to who they're loyal to, if it's not fitting their equation, that loyalty isn't to you.

That's just the reality of it as he saw firsthand. A niggah's loyalty is as good a niggah's presence. You peep dudes in general together all of the time, road dog type shit and thick as thieves. Dudes getting rabbs together, whether they were jacking or slanging work. Banging together, bussing and squabbling niggahs down together, going against the grain together. Y'all are in the turf together, hitting turf functions together and fuck with turf rats together, something y'all are known for by homies. Here it is, a niggah's wrapped up and been wrapped up. The cold thing about it, the niggahs that told on the homie is still in the turf even after it went viral. Straight hanging out. "Ain't that about a bitch!" What type of shit is that though? Still coming around, still hanging out in the turf, still allowed to (SMH) and he's posting on the block, seeing this bitch made niggah on a daily basis, if not weekly. Shenanigans I'll tell you (SMH). Don't be surprised if he isn't hanging out in the turf on a daily, wow! What type of shit these dudes on though? Where are these dudes' loyalty at? If not for me, at for the game. "A snitch is a snitch, he's putting a black eye in the game and y'all "around him" (seeing him), knowing he's foul (SMH).

What's up with dude? A dude you're fucking with and running with on a daily. A'ight, the rest of those dudes aren't on no loyalty shit. They didn't run the streets with us, they didn't hustle with us, they didn't buss with us, they didn't bang with us, they didn't squabble with us, they didn't hang wit us, it was us. What's up with your loyalty? What type of shit you're on? If don't nobody else have me, you're supposed to. It just says a lot about dudes, and how fake they are. Had a loyal dude in me and I was messing with you. But yeah, that type of shit is crazy as fuck, but it goes on, dudes are actually messing with these snitch ass dudes though. Blowing with them, drinking with them, hanging out with them, chopping it up with them and all of that.

    Dudes don't have no type of loyalty whatsoever. These are the type of dudes were affiliated with and are socializing with and don't find out til its all bad. That's what it came to, it shouldn't take a dude to get wrapped up, that you messed with though, and on a daily to say you need to holler at the rat bastard. (SMH) Dudes know the dude's foul and he got down foul. Everyone in the turf and is a somebody knows this dude isn't cool (SMH). It should already be a done deal on that dude, should've been voted off the island. First off, how are you dudes even fucking with this dude? As a matter of fact, ask yourself how does that work? Explain that to a dude. All I'm seeing are dudes condoning snitchism and being complicit in allowing them to hang out (SMH). Then when a dude gets at homies and shoots that paperwork its like, "Don't trip, homie, that's as good as handled, we got you!" Then its like, "On the turf, that's going to get handled, on such and such rest in peace!" That shit isn't good as handled and a niggah ain't got no mutha fuckin body. Turf and the dead homie blew the fuck up, kabooooom!!! Here it is 5, 6 years after the fact. It's no bueno. Shit still isn't handled. He was still hearing how this dude's

## FEELING SOME TYPE OF WAY—SODO AUSTIN

in the turf, basically ain't ever left. But we're supposed to be dudes though. Just crazy to me and burnt out. I guess it is what it is though. Loyal dudes are a dying breed. Don't get me wrong, there's loyal dudes still, they're just a rare breed.

Dudes are selling the ranch, taking their batteries out, leaving dudes for dead. You name it, dudes are doing it (SMH). A lot of dudes aren't worth being loyal to and aren't worthy of a dude's loyalty. Some we give our loyalty to don't deserve it. I've ran into many dudes speaking on this very situation and sentiments. In the county jail and in the maze, dudes are like wow. It's shitty as a mutha fucka! My last cellie I just had from Harlem Crip was just speaking on this situation, feeling like, "If dudes aren't being bought off for crumbs, b'cuz dudes are out there thirsty as fuck, on some dehydration type shit." And are like, "Fuck that, I ain't trying to be sitting in that mutha fucka with nan niggah!"

Behind this dude feeling like somebody's going to tell on them. We pretty much concluded, dudes loyalties are fucked up and aren't worth a fuck. Knowing yourself, if the Chuck was on the other foot, you would've handled that wax. Dudes loyalty for the most part is fucked up and on some Mickey ass shit. That's just the bottom line. The cloth they were cut from was watered down and bullshit, whoever laced them. Didn't lace a dude right. Dudes don't know what it is to be loyal and I can bang that. As I had said, loyalty isn't part-time. How are you going to pick and choose when to be loyal and what to be loyal to when it's a dude you're messing with though. Not just mess with you, but mess with you on a daily, bending corners. That shit is Mickey, that shit you're doing isn't loyalty, it's disloyal. You're whole get down is garbage. Some say you can't learn loyalty, it has to be in a dude or a bitch already. That whole scenario though, is burnt out. Now it really makes me wonder how many dudes were bagged or have been wrapped up. And who they were loyal to, were they really loyal?

At what price does loyalty come and does it even come then? Since I'm already speaking on jail, I might as well use this instance too. Mind you, these are your dudes. Or you dude you were in traffic with on a daily basis, getting it in as only you did. Your boy though. When you were first wrapped up in the beginning and you were in the county, homies were at you and fucking with you. Putting rabbs on your books, you could call collect to several spots, logging in where homies are posted at, or there was rabbs on the phone and you could just "log in" (call). It seems, though, as soon as a dude get sentenced, whether he was "banged over the head" (got football numbers plus) or not, and waiting to "catch the chain" (taking that bus ride to the maze), they start falling off. Shit starts getting Mickey and in comes the "funnies" (games, lying and distancing). Mutha fucka's start having jokey jokes, a dude's bitch too (SMH). Should've saw that coming though.

Whore bags aren't loyal, she's immediately coming with the funnies and the bullshit, so she can distance herself and go fuck out of both pant legs and be the whore bag she wanted to be. Technically, she was already a whore bag, she was just on the low with her whore bagness (SMH). It's like everything shuts down all at once. It's not all at once, though, it plays out gradually over the course of a few months, sometimes sooner. If the phone doesn't have a block on it, it's the number change or the disconnect. (SMH) Before any of those scenarios play out, you would try to call but all of a sudden you can't ever catch anyone. You can't catch your bitch, homies or so-called family. The homie might be one that will reconnect once you get to the maze, maybe a bitch, or possibly a so-called family member, big "might," big "maybe," big "possibly." Even if they do it's not going to last long. Mutha fuckas will "break wide on you" (leave/disappear), quick, fast and in a hurry.

    You may, might or possibly get a little "run" out of them (doing things for you, might even get a visit). Consisting of receiving a few dots and dashes here and there, maybe some rabbs, big maybe, once or twice, a few captured moments here and there. Maybe a package and it's a "wrap" (over with), suuuper dunzo! That's the extent of their loyalty. Then it's the "lay down" (done with the situation), nobody's trying to pull up no more, homies, bitches or so-called family, no bueno! But there's supposed to be homies, this raggedy ass bitch supposed to be my bitch and they're supposed to be a niggah's family. Who you were basically willing to put yours on the line for, out of loyalty (SMH). Being a loyal mutha fucka, then finding out they weren't when it was all said and done is foul. That's a cold reality check for a dude's ass. What dude isn't going to be in his "feels" and feeling some type of way? Or be bitter as fuck! A niggah like me is bitter and salty, I'm on my suuuper fuck you tip!, with homies, so-called family and raggedy ass bitches! It's like a mutha fucka's getting slapped in the face or spit on. On a gang of different occasions a dude was

## FEELING SOME TYPE OF WAY—SODO AUSTIN

down with you, came to your aid or assisted you. Down with you and for you. When you needed a dude, he was there. All you had to do was call.

Call and he'll come running b'cuz that's what loyal dudes do. What loyal bitches and family supposed to do, who you've been there for at some point, who you've supported on different levels of support. When you were needed, you were there based on your loyalty to them, as it is with you, but this is the thanks a dude gets though. You forgot about all we've been through, downplay it or disregarded it. Forgot about how tight and cool we were, forgot about how we got rabbs on the block together, how we were gang gang together, how we fucked turf rats, bussed at enemigos, banged mutha fuckas and squabbled niggahs together huh? Don't none of that mean shit, the interest is no longer there. It's easy to disregard the history. With so-called family and bitches too. It was all gravity just a week ago.

How soon they forget, quick, fast and in a hurry, as if shit never existed with you or between you, trying to distance and separate themselves (SMH). As far as she's concerned, even though a dude was doing and being him, he was still doing her. See, you can do you as long as you're doing them (her). That's just on some loyal shit, niggahs are gon be niggahs! At the end of the day, she acts like she never said she loved you and she'll always love you and care about you. Like she never said she'll always fuck with you regardless (I'm speaking on BM's, wives and situationships). Bitch isn't doing nothing but "popping it" (just talking, it isn't meant), telling a dude what she thinks he wants to hear "at that moment" (having a common interest and being on some dick and pussy shit). It was never lies. But you know its only good and lasts while you're a presence and dicking her silly ass down, sliding her a few rabbs to make it make sense. Bitches act like you weren't there for their dusty ass when it counted or was needed.

They're working with that selective memory, only remembering what fits her narrative (SMH). A dude isn't saying you owe a dude shit, b'cuz he didn't do what he done to be reimbursed, it was done out of loyalty, outside of playing his part and position. That's just crazy though, how you can lay down and leave a niggahs for dead, as if there were never an existence. As for homies, you know a dude was loyal and loyal to the soil, and had you without a doubt, always sagging it out and would. Based on a dude's loyalty to you as a real homie, I would've never laid down on you or left you for dead, especially if the Chuck was on the other foot. Clearly our loyalties weren't one in the same. However, there's another side to loyalty, where as he knows the mutha fuckas in his circle and around him.

Using that to advantage, so he stays having conflicts and getting into Mickey situations, knowing he can make that call, dudes are pulling up and with the shenanigans...tripping! Off the dribble, feeling some type of way. You're into something, they're into something. Dudes are on some Mickey shit with you, they're into some Mickey shit with them. So every time you look around, he's getting into some type of situation. It's always the next niggah's drama, but there you go going to their aid regardless of what it is, that's how loyalty gets down and what it looks like. Being a

## FEELING SOME TYPE OF WAY—SODO AUSTIN

dude who's really about loyalty and to a fault, I'm not going to ever let the next bullshit mutha fucka deter me or have me switch up on my being loyal, that's who I am. Especially behind a few bad seeds.

I'm not going to change who I am or what I'm about, b'cuz you aren't who you said you were, with a character flaw of the worse kind. Yeah, do you though. I feel you but check it out though. Don't think b'cuz you have niggahs that'll push with you, you can just run around getting into it with dudes, just based on. That's no bueno! Knowing you have homies who have your six and are going to sag it out with you, balls out. That shit isn't straight and isn't ever cool being a bozo on some bozo shit! Don't fuck around and get your license revoked, fucking around! That shit ain't ever straight, you could get homies in a wreck, coming to your rescue on some bullshit and you know homies are coming.

Dudes don't recognotice none of that though. They can't recollect shit if it doesn't fit their narrative. That shit could come back and haunt a niggah, not just them but you too. A few years ago I was with a homie in Ironwood, he was a laid back and quiet homie, the homie "S-Bad" and easy to get along with, real cool homie, cool as a fan and was gang gang. But you know the quiet type, rather be felt than heard, ain't nothing wrong with that though. The homie loved the turf, loved the homies, loved having that presence. He pretty much stayed to himself, but did stay fucking with the homies. A real solid and straight homie though, but a loyal niggah too. That's what he was and loyal to a fault. Yeah, one of

## FEELING SOME TYPE OF WAY—SODO AUSTIN

those dudes (I.I.P. homie). It was an honor to have met you and known you.

We used to chop it up a lot on a daily, "spinning laps" (walking them) on the track, on the yard, in the maze. Just walking, talking and talking in the scenery around us, that's what we done. He was on his way back to the bricks. At that point the homie was about a month away from being resurrected. When he did finally push back out there he got bagged within a few months of being out. His loyalty being to a fault got him bagged behind a dude to me wasn't worthy the homie's loyalty, not at all. Based on his realness and loyalty to dudes he fucked with, homies or not. If he messed with you like that, he was loyal to you and the relationship. The dude he was extending his loyalty to was bagged too.

Loyalty does have its drawbacks and it does have back looks. Homies are just on, "I'm gon be there for my niggahs, that's it, that's all." Loyalty, though, too isn't trying to hump on your boy's bitch, even if she's a whore bag trying to throw the pussy at you. That's still a can't do and an "Ain't gon be able to do it," then you put your boy up on his bitch's shenanigans. Put him up on his bitch get down, letting him know what type of bitch he got. Another instance of loyalty, say a homie got you on your feet, you didn't have shit and was doing bad. He put you in the game and you get your weight up. Somehow the dude who put you on fall off for whatever reason. He takes a major loss and can't get back. But now you're up...up! Suuuper up! You're not going to forget how you got to where you are, even if he wasn't looking for nothing back.

## FEELING SOME TYPE OF WAY—SODO AUSTIN

But based on, though, he fell off, a loyal niggah's going to pull up on him with something to get him back going. He has that coming. If it was me, I'm going to make sure he's right. He got me eating at the end of the day. Blowing bomb kush, drinking good, riding in a few different swoops on hunnid spokes. Living good, geared up, jewelry pieces up, taking care of my bay bays and a few other whore bags with bomb pussy and bomb head. Have to keep that bomb shit locked in, for sure. Why I couldn't see him with that assist? That's what I can do. Do, easy call. It's an easy ass call for me personally, being loyal. Being a loyal dude, you can and will reach back, seeing a niggah with it to get him back on his feet.

Why wouldn't you want to, though? Anything less than "looking back" is a mis-overstanding. This is the dude that put you on and got you right. Now you're getting it in, doing you and how you should be doing you. Feel me, though? He has you eating, how you're eating, by letting you in so you can eat. But the cold thing about it, though, you actually have dudes that wouldn't and would be on some shit like, "That's on that niggah, ain't got shit to do with me, I ain't ask that niggah to bless me, he done that on his own." Then it's like, "I don't owe a mutha fucka shit!" (SMH) To me, that's some disloyal ass shit. You don't even have loyalty for the game. First off, if the niggah fell off and you know that was the case, you shouldn't even have to ask, it should be an automatic, the reason he fell off is trivial. Loyalty is everything, whether you're in the streets or in the maze.

# FEELING SOME TYPE OF WAY—SODO AUSTIN

Chapter 12

"Groundwork"

Now groundwork, my dude, is a whole different element. It's essential with any successful outcome. You basically have to do it to get that successful look and outcome, anything less you're prone to have a fucked up outcome b'cuz shit's going to turn out Mickey, based on. Based on your not having done your groundwork. Nowadays you can't just be all willy nilly with shit or about shit, straight up. You can never just up and do things, you'll find yourself wrapped up, banged or bagged, it's imminent. Imminence knocking at a mutha fucka's door. Knock knock knock! Shit, we all have to live with being out there like that. You can never just up and do shit on a whim, you're leaving the door open for failure to walk in, feel me, too many variables that can come into play. Bluey bluey. You always have to be mindful of the fact there's a bigger captured moment, it's about preservation.

Depending on what the situation is, it could be detrimental to a niggah, death or being wrapped the fuck up. As I've said, these days niggahs can't just up and do things without doing your groundwork. Hold up, I'll regardless to what the fuck it is. You have to do it, it's not ever negotiable, that's simply a must. I mean, if you're about your B.I. and you're on it. Why expose yourself to the bullshit dudes when you don't have to? Why go half assed at something when you can take preventative measures and appropriate steps to ensure your outcome is successful? Why be half assed about things, I'm just saying though. If a dude puts thought into doing things, why not take the time to wait it out and see it through?

Sometimes things cost more than what a dude is willing to pay real talk. That time you take out to do the groundwork will be well worth it and I can bang that. It'll be the difference, it'll make the difference at the end of the day. Your mission or objective having a better chance at being manifested on a better standing is what it comes down to and the less likely chance of things going Mickey for a dude. I'm quite sure we all would like good results from that which we step to and seeking benefits. Who wouldn't want to be on top and that's what the intended was off the dribble? So why not better the chances doing your groundwork, the ins and outs, the dos and not to dos, the like this and the like thats? Feel me though? A dude has to be on point.

Ain't shit "fly" (cool) about half assing. Thats how a dude comes up on the short end of a situation and it's a bad look. If you're trying to make it count, make it make sense, when it comes to you trying to get your issue. Get it, just get it right and be mindful of the elements and be mindful of your elements. If you're trying to do and be you, do it one way and that's the right way. Don't step to anything blindly and without the appropriate intel, b'cuz can't nothing come from that look but a bad look. Intel is definitely essential in a dude's outcome. I'm sure you're familiar with the adage "You get back what you put in." It's said for a reason, you put in nothing, you get nothing, straight up! You go at something half assed. You're basically setting yourself up for a failure at the end of the day. You're not going to gAin't shit "fly" (cool) about half assing. Thats how a dude comes up on the short end of a situation and it's a bad look. If you're trying to make it count, make it make sense, when it comes to you trying to get your issue. Get it, just get it right and be mindful of the elements and be mindful of your elements. If you're trying to do and be you, do it one way and that's the right way. Don't step to anything blindly and without the appropriate intel, b'cuz can't nothing come from that look but a bad look. Intel is definitely essential in a dude's outcome. I'm sure you're familiar with the adage "You get back what you put in." It's said for a reason, you put in nothing, you get nothing, straight up! You go at something half assed. You're basically setting yourself up for a failure at the end of the day. You're not going to get what you anticipated and I can bang that, that's just keeping it one hunnid with you, success won't fit your equation, period. You simply gets nothing, not a damn thing.et what you anticipated and I can bang that, that's just keeping it one hunnid with you, success won't fit your equation, period. You simply gets nothing, not a damn thing.

    Not doing your groundwork is putting in nothing next to a guaranteed failure, though you can get the "E" for effort, but fuck that! Why set yourself up, that's a minus. Dude, doing your groundwork is for your benefit, for the most part, b'cuz it's something that's going to benefit you or your push. If you're willing to step up to the plate, as I said, make shit count and add up. Why just settle for the effort when you can be proactive and instrumental in the outcome. But can you honestly say you really gave it an effort and shot your shot? Not giving yourself the best chance is doing yourself a disservice. Not doing your groundwork isn't

## FEELING SOME TYPE OF WAY—SODO AUSTIN

giving yourself that edge or leg up to win. You're not giving yourself that look to accomplish what it is you need to accomplish.

A'ight, trip, getting to the instances, for instance, you're trying to hit a lick and pass (come up). It's a spot you want to lick, say it's a dope spot and you know dudes have it booming and it's making suuuper rabbs up in there. You just can't push up in the mutha fucka all willy nilly and lay it down, that's no bueno! It doesn't work like that, but it's a good way to get your ass banged. It isn't meant to work like that and isn't supposed to work like that, but what's so crazy, niggahs ain't stupid enough to run that but they're arrogant enough. For one, a mutha fucka don't know in the slightest how many heads are up in there. If they have dogs, if they have cameras, you don't know, too many variables. You don't know shit, not a thing and that's how dudes get their mental brought to them, his "matter" (brain, guts, etc.) all over the walls or on the floor. Doing shit blind or going about shit blindly. Your subject to get wrapped up or have an all praise is due Allah and to Allah we belong and to him we return moment.

Get your mind around that look, I'm just saying. It's reality, it ain't an illusion of truth wearing a mask of deception well. For two, you don't know if dudes have bangers up in the spot. Not at all. All spots don't, but don't count on that or assume that assumptions aren't going to keep you safe or your "beans" (brains) in your head (SMH). When that goes Mickey, you're going to fuck around and be on the wrong end of the equation, when the smoke settles. But to be safe you need to know, for that matter, a niggah don't know when its the best time to pull up. Just the other day me and a homie were speaking on an instance somewhat related. The homie was basically saying if he pushed (went) to a spot to get some trees and he sees a dude that doesn't look like he would resist or try to get active, he's coming back the ski mask way, masked up and with a banger to see what as niggah's working with.

He never said he was going to check the spot out first. He's just on some "I'mma go back masked up." Don't know shit, I'm just up in there. For three, you don't know who watching the spot. All a dude know is, you peeped a gang of traffic and it's rabbs up in there (SMH), horseplaying! Thats all of the intel you have. You don't know shit and that's not knowing shit, nothing more than a dude just said. And you probably got what info you do have from a homie or put up on it from a homie, that isn't saying or knowing much (SMH). He's all amped up on some extra'ed shit, animated too. "Cuz, it's up in there, we can get it, niggahs can be got, we can get them!...Blood, it's up in there, all we got to do is pull up. We can get it, I'm telling you, niggahs can be got!" Slow your roll Turbo! True, dudes can be got, no doubt about it, nobody above it, any mutha fucka can be got. Will be got, have been got! In some instances should be got!, just being on some Gilligan shit.

That part right there, I'm on some Bitterchild advocate type shit. Dudes can be got, but you have to go about it right or take the off chance that they're slipping like that up in that mutha fucka, just pushing up in there all willy nilly and it's Mickey. Then you're basically finding out otherwise it wasn't what a niggah thought it was. Reality's a mutha fucka! Finding out it wasn't like that, not at all, stupid! (SMH)

## FEELING SOME TYPE OF WAY—SODO AUSTIN

Just being on some cocky and arrogant shit will cost a dude his life, it's not going to be a good look. Why jeopardize yourself or your boy(s)? Unnecessary! Cameras can be watching you the whole fucking time, looks can be deceiving. Just know and overstand that, that goes back to the illusion of truth wearing a mask of deception well. Niggahs could easily be setting up crash test dummies and here you come being the crash test dummy. Dudes do and are setting up crash test dummies b'cuz dudes are sleep and they know dudes are sleep (SMH) Autobot! They're sleep, thinking the next dude is sleep, not being mindful of the fact, some are but not all are. Can't think that way, period. No bueno on that! Don't ever assume that every dude is sleep and run with that b'cuz it's basically a false sense of security on your part.

You think you have "the up" (advantage) on dudes when in reality you don't and dudes have "the up" on you. A'ight, just say you did get up in there and ain't shit up in there, then what? Wasted energy, time and you jeopardize yourself for nothing (SMH). It's shit you need to do your groundwork on. It's no different from flocking or trying to run up in a "B.I.", the same applies. You still have to do your groundwork, checking for cameras, the entrances, the exits, the exit route, nosy neighbors, etc. How many heads you're dealing with. What the traffic's like, or look like, or might look like the day of. Therefore, you know when the shit's straight and when it isn't, fuck all the willy nilly shit, that'll get you bagged or banged. You're basically just ensuring you're results are straight opposed to them being Mickey b'cuz shit went sideways and you're having an imminent moment. You're looking for that win, which is the whole reason you got out there like that. I'm not saying put yourself out there like that. I'm just saying if you're already out there like that, do your groundwork, don't be on no goofball shit. Make it count, make it add up. Don't get active on a whim or just feel b'cuz you're "heated" (armed), it's an automatic, it's going to go right. That isn't ever the case, so you know and overstand. B'cuz you have a lot of weighing against you by not knowing what you're up against, by not knowing the whole get down. It's just so much that can go crooked than not go crooked. The groundwork isn't ever to be rushed, should be rushed. You have to take your time, it's not a race for time but a marathon for safety. You shouldn't want to be rushed. You're moving too fast. Moving too fast comes with being careless and with carelessness comes crookedness. Something to think about though. Be sure to be thorough with your shit, make everything add up and make it count.

  Your thoroughness will ensure the chances of your success. A dude being half assed isn't going to get it done, not at all! But it will definitely get you banged, bagged or wrapped up. That's what it will get a niggah. As I had previously said, you don't just up and do shit without thought, hesitation or investigation. That groundwork is the grey print and the very foundation to a dude's coming out on T.O.P., which is the objective, coming out on top. 9 out of 10, those that don't or didn't do their groundwork found themselves twisted up like a pretzel and assed the fuck out. I'm not saying that it's the case in all cases, some dudes do get lucky, but the deck is stacked against them, they just chose to shoot their shot. The odds were against them, the unseen, the unknown and the possibility of shit going crooked, based on the unexpected. The unexpected of some kind.

The "two-eleven" turned into a "one-eighty-seven." Wow, who expected that look though? Certainly not you, if that wasn't a part of the get down. But that's just how crooked shit can go unexpectedly, that and you're jeopardizing your own safety and freedom. The whole thing is not being in an uncertain or uncontrolled situation. It's not ever a good look. You want it to be but it's not about what you want horseplaying! "Bloom...bloom...bloom...blop...blop...blop!" Yeah, a dude's up out of there, doing it moving stage left. A dude is limiting the likely chance of some Mickey shit happening, nothing is for sure or a hunnid percent. But you can makes your odds and percentage favorable, going in the direction you want shit to go in. That's what you can do by just doing the groundwork. It's not just the "traffic" (street) aspect of it, it's applied in B.I. too. You're just not going to up and invest your rabbs into something you know nothing about, I don't see it. You're going to find out about that B.I., its growth potential, the returns, its pluses, its minuses, its positives, its negatives, location, clientele, etc.

If you just up and invest and know nothing about what you're investing in, you might as well trick off the rabbs, why not? Fuck it, get some pussy or some head out of the deal. Some drink, some trees, or whatever else you're into, I'm just saying. Aye, it's a lot, but why not capitalize on it, make it count, make it add up, make it make sense. At least you're winning going that route. Shit, if you can make it make sense, it's a win. If you're just fucking off, why not make it and have it make sense. Make it count. It's always the same, you have to do your groundwork, period. It's success, stack the deck in your favor. Ensure your success, ensure your better odds. Learn all there is to learn about the look and about what it is dude's stepping to, fuck being in the blind or being on some whim type shit, you know. You have to do your due diligence, that's just the bottom line when you're committing yourself to shit, especially when it's some shit that can cost you. Whether it's on a positive note or on a negative note, that's just being Bitterchild advocate. For those concerned, I'm not promoting anything. I'm just keeping it a hunnid and letting someone know the importance of doing their groundwork with anything they're approaching.

    Doing their groundwork and not being on no false sense of security type shit, b'cuz without groundwork you're ensuring a failure and the deck being stacked when it's already stacked, if you're just keeping it a hunnid. You're just opening the door for shit to go crooked. Ensuring the opposite of what your main objective was, blowing up your push. Again, it's the grey print, it's your guide, it's the foundation and the difference between a good look and a bad look, the very essence of your success or failure. I'm not an expert on the subject at hand, but I feel I can address it based on my experience and based on my exposures on both instances, the success and the failure aspect of it. Me personally, I've had licks go straight and were good looks. Break bread or fake dead!

    With doing the groundwork though, not being on the willy nilly shit. But before I started doing my groundwork and looking into shit, shit used to really go all bad for the most part, went straight crooked. So I

## FEELING SOME TYPE OF WAY—SODO AUSTIN

know a thing or 3 about groundwork and what groundwork can and will do, and the effect I can and will have on a situation. The difference between it being Mickey or straight. Simply put, dudes have to handle their wax and don't play with it. Can't let the wax handle you. I've been bussed at b'cuz a mutha fucka done shit on a whim or simply b'cuz a homie told me about a lick and I pushed on some goofball shit. Basically, putting my life in their hands, which is what I was doing, not knowing homies didn't know the B.I., just took their word for it. Took their word for it to be what they said it was, never a good look... East Side!

The groundwork was never done and just had me on some "Let's try some shit!", type lick. A fuck it, we're going to shoot our shot. Being honest, that shit ain't cool at all. I was horseplaying! It could've been bluey bluey! I could've blamed nobody but T.I.C.! I could've easily been on some, "Hol up homie, what's the B.I. with that look!" Instead of just "pushing" (going). Sometimes niggahs push off speculation, and speculation will have a dude fucked off, just like assumptions will have a dude fucked off, sometimes fucked over. Being surprised ain't ever straight! Not when you're dealing with shit that can bag you, get you banged or wrapped up. Shit gets hectic, gets real. Get real hectic quick like. Some instances, some of the licks went straight, but knowing what a niggah know now, I can't play that game, no bueno! I was playing, for certain (SMH).

I can't see myself running up in shit without knowing the B.I. But that's the old me, I'm cool on all of that. Been there done that, over it! That's just a cold game to be playing, fuck all that, it ain't going down. I ain't going to be able to do it. That's just out, my dude, I'm not trying to get bagged, banged or wrapped up... I'm straight. Especially if I can get out from under this life sentence. Yeah, 211's got a niggah booked! Certified jacker! I don't have to get bagged, banged or wrapped the fuck up. I ain't trying to have no parts of it if I don't have to and that just some real ass shit, real as real can and going to get. B'cuz at the end of the day a niggah's a realist, strictly about real things and real situations. Been wrapped up twice and I'm wrapped up now, was almost bagged on a few occasions and have almost been banged on a few occasions on that same type of bullshit.

Just up and doing shit on a whim, all willy nilly and not knowing the B.I. Those are 3 surefire ways to get twisted without a doubt. Especially letting a homie come to you and you're just taking his word for what and as it is, on some goofball shit. As if that business is the business and fuck it. Shit, for all a niggah know, it could be all Mickey, who's to say? All he (the homie) know and going by are you being thirsty and on some thirsty shit and basically down for whatever. Know you'll be with it and be with getting the rabbs, he just don't tell you everything he knows he should b'cuz he knows if he does, you might not want to push.

He isn't going to feel that look, so to ensure you're with it, he's going to put some extras on it to get you to bite. Put a 10 on a 2 (SMH). Making it sound good, so off you bounce and there you go. All in the dark, all willy nilly, not knowing a damn thing. At that point whatever happens is going to happen, it applies to the "work" game too, you're trying to open up a spot, you have to find the right location. Know who the neighbors are, as far as them being the type to mind their B.I., not tripping off you or what you have going on, with all of that traffic all throughout the day and night, spot booming, or will they be the type that will trip, being quick to call "the Ones"? The area in general, is it an area or block the Ones push through constantly? These are things a dude has to investigate and know. Investigating and doing your groundwork, it can be the end of a beginning, or a beginning of an end. Only you can decide the final result of that course and look, keeping it a hunnid.

Whims are merely impulses a mutha fucka can't really afford to be moving on, especially deriving from where they're deriving from, which is that impulsive act. Often illogical notions which have consequences should shit go sideways or Mickey, that sideways and Mickey shit is failure. What is failure? Riddle me that though homie. To me, it's a dude dropping the ball and fumbling (SMH). Basically to sum it up it's bad B.I., don't let not doing your groundwork be the reason, feel me? B'cuz again, doing the groundwork you can't go sideways. How can you go wrong or sideways? Riddle me that one too. Knowing the situation and task at hand, regardless of what it might be. How can a mutha fucka go wrong having firsthand knowledge of what it is you're stepping into that grey print, bettering the chances of a dude's success?

Bettering the chances b'cuz you're putting a distance between yourself and failure. In the streets failure isn't an option due to the cost if it, jail, possibly death (being bagged) or banged. "2" you can't possibly come back from "1." You can't, but their all imminent. In the event you do though, get to bounce back from it, let experience and exposure tighten your hand up, if a niggah's fortunate enough to avoid the "lotto ticket" (life). In B.I. you just cut your losses and come anew. I mean, that's a better look when it's all said and done, you know? Cutting your losses and coming anew, you can come back, you still have action on some get back on that option and a presence. You just lost your rabbs, your time and your effort, no biggy! At least it wasn't a niggah's life, by jail or death, feel me? Do you, but do you the right way. Don't half ass do you, if that's what it is, that's all I'm saying. A dude has to allow himself to win off the dribble. Like that shit Charlie Sheen was hollering...winning!

A niggah has to allow himself to win and come out on top of the pile. A dude can't start out the gate with the odds against him. Have to put the odds in your favor. If the deck has to be stacked, let the deck be stacked in your favor. Anything less is a mis-overstanding. Give yourself the better odds, being odds are in play, fuck the silly and dumb shit. Bullshit ain't never about nothing, nothing at all you know. Keep in mind, "I have to do that groundwork b'cuz if I don't, I'm opening myself up to some bullshit jumping off." I'm quite sure though, I'd dudes would've thought to have done the groundwork, those that are put in situations before they got into the situation would have. No doubt in a dude's mind, that's what would've taken place b'cuz I can pretty much guarantee a niggah after some shit happened. That wasn't encountered or put into the equation, in came the "what ifs."

The "could of's," the "should of's," or the "Damn, what if I would've done this shit like this or like that?" Or "Only if I would've done

## FEELING SOME TYPE OF WAY—SODO AUSTIN

it the other way I started to." "Damn, I could've done it like this, that or the third?" "Why didn't I do it like this instead of like that?" (SMH) "Why didn't I follow my first mind?" "Damn, I should've done this or that!" Second guessing your decision or choice. But you know what? By that time it's already "acted on" (said or done). Over with, dunzo, a done deal, cancel Christmas. That chapter's closed, stick a mutha fuckin fork in it podnah! D.O.N.E.! I'm just saying, it's a wrap and it is what it is. You can't put yourself out there and shit's not right on your end, you're asking for some shit to come into play b'cuz can't nothing come of it good.

Too many things can go wrong and come out way crooked. A dude isn't trying to take that ride, that's my energy...flag on the play. If a dude don't have to, why would he? Riddle me that. When all it takes is for a dude to do his "homework" (groundwork). It's simple mathematics, one plus one is two, all day long. I know my math is up to par. It might take a minute to do your investigation, but the time you took out will be worth the time, especially if it's going to keep you from getting yourself in a mutha fuckin wreck, bagged, banged or wrapped the fuck up like a burrito from Chimas (a Mexican eating spot on 10th and Alamitos in the City) (Long Beach, California).

Straight caught up, a bad look by all accounts. At the end of the day, somebody's going to be feeling some type of way. I know a dude can feel that, you can't help but to feel it. It's some real shit, you know how I've been getting it in these chapters, real things, real situations, raw and uncut. It's going to make a major difference, taking that out to know what's

## FEELING SOME TYPE OF WAY—SODO AUSTIN

what, whereas it's going to make sense and can make sense, do make sense. How shit works, supposed to work, who's coming, who's going. What time this or that takes place? When it's a good time to "push" or "press play." Does the spot have cameras? Where are the best routes to take. Leaving or coming. Can a dude actually get away without being detected? Would a dude actually get away? Is everything adding up to a dude mentally? Is one and one two? Is two and two four?

    Is this, that and the third angle covered? This is some shit you have to ask yourself and can answer yourself with the utmost of confidence. Are you straight with what you've learned? Are you good with it? If you're not, who's going to be? Can't nobody do it for you. Do you think you've learned enough? Do you think more could be or could've been learned? Ultimately, though, are you content with what you've learned, are you satisfied? Can you say you're willing to take that step, take that giant leap forward? Are your bases covered? These are the questions a dude has to ask himself confidently. If you can, then do what you do...handle your wax!

    The main thing, though, you can say confidently is you've done your groundwork and you gave yourself the opportunity to win and get your shine on. That's the main thing and your bottom line is allowing yourself a chance to come out on top for the most part. Though always mindful of audibles in the middle of a play. Shit happens. You can prepare and plan, but shit doesn't always go as prepared or planned. Life is suuuper funny that way. It's never a dude's intent to self detonate, setting himself up for a failure or to fail. By the same token, though, a dude has to put himself in a straight position. Anything else, he's horseplaying, which is a mis-overstanding. Remember too, if you were trying to push, you and you alone have to bite that bullet. Can't fault nobody and ain't nobody going to ride that, that's all you. It's like a mutha fucka's always saying, you pick your own poison. It is what it is, and going to be, what it's going to be, period, point blank. But yeah, that's about the size of it though. You know? Well, the importance of groundwork had been said and painted as vivid as it could be.

As vivid as it could be coming from me. Based on my experiences and exposures. So I know groundwork and overstand it. As I overstand the importance of it. I definitely know what gives you a better chance at succeeding...doing your homework. I wanted to present you that better look at shit, as it was with me, by the various instances and situations, by way of directing your thought process in that general direction, having you mindful and aware. Though some of us know, some of us don't know or don't care to and that's why there's a lot of dudes find themselves bagged, banged or wrapped up (SMH). That's a result of having a case of the "fuck its!" (SMH) For those though, that do know, it's just saying the importance of it and the relevance of it, you know? I know how it is to not do what's necessary to "get to it" (handle your business). For dudes that don't, I'm trying to expose you to what I've been exposed to, how and why. As I've experienced them. What worked and what didn't.

As well as the importance and relevance, therefore it can be exercised or considered in one's endeavors regardless of the "play"

## FEELING SOME TYPE OF WAY—SODO AUSTIN

(situation). Do with this information what you will, take it and run with it or not. However, it's in the air, as I put it up there. Make it do what it do! Or stay with the "fuck its!", shooting your shot. It's your failure or it's your success at the end of the day. Whichever you're pushing play on, that's your fly zone. I tried relaying it as simple as I possibly could and with toning down the "slang" (Ebonics) (SMH), which my guy Hoover Lon got at me about. Sometimes I can get carried away b'cuz I know the way I speak, I like to write trying to be so relatable to my target audience. But at the same time having to be mindful and overstanding the fact that everyone isn't going to able to relate, so I found the common ground that works, while maintaining that level of being me as only I could.

I can only hope you've thoroughly enjoyed not only this chapter but the entire Feeling Some Type Of Way. Do overstand and know moving forward, you'll always get the authentic me and dealing with strictly real things and real situations, from the streets to the maze.

# FEELING SOME TYPE OF WAY—SODO AUSTIN

"Outroduction"

In conclusion, "Feeling Some Type Of Way" is merely my "feelings and emotions towards situations inside and outside of the maze" from the "pen" (prison) to the "streets." My "views" and "thoughts" are vast when it comes to "real things" and "real situations." As with how I address and express myself, while trying to be as vivid and raw as humanly possible. It's always my intentions to be felt, as only I can be, in a way I'm "overstood" and "related to." In return, I make no apologies for my brashness or bitterness. I'll always remain real and true with myself, my F and E's, and with those who've become a fan of Sodo Austin and will give nothing less than what you've come to expect from me as a fan...always! If it's not in the "paint" it's not "Sodo!"

Which I set the standard for in "Yard Life" (Exposé, Real Life Inside Of Prison). It's my lane in general, which translate through the way that I write, which is with purpose, as I'd expressed to my author liaison Frank Reuter. My purpose is and always will be to share my experiences, situations, choices and exposures as they were and are with me, in my life, being in and from the streets to the pen, as only I can and without having to be watered down, censored or compromised, thus allowing myself to remain fully engaged, exposed and vulnerable to mouths of "Gilligan critics," "haters" and "Autobots" alike from inside and outside of the maze.

Putting high value on my range to do and be me, I can care less about who's feeling some type of way. Your feelings aren't my concern b'cuz it's not about you or your feelings, but about me expressing and stressing mine, through any and all of my nonfiction efforts, which I hope'll be thoroughly enjoyed by all that encounter my work. Being respected for what and as it is, as it pertains to the street life and pertains to prison life, on the yard, strictly real things and real situations, which is what "Feeling Some Type Of Way" represents as with "Yard Life" (Exposé, Real Life Inside Of Prison), nothing less than real things and real situations. It's what I represent as a "Bitterchild" (a person bitter about past and present situations) and represent in general standing on reality. And in reality, when it comes to life and life's situations dealing with individuals, circumstances and relationships, on both sides of the wall...

I try to deal with all of the above, but one way, and that's always the right way, even when it's complicated or hard to do. Overstanding our plans, though, are constantly stagnated by forces beyond our control, for the most part, it's just what it is. But multiple times I've been frustrated by the "zigs and zags" of the streets and on the yards I've walked on. Individuals forget about what you said, they forget about what you do, but they won't forget about how a dude feel in his forward momentum. I recognotice my selfishness, my being impatient, my insecurities, my mistakes I've made, as I recognotice my being out of control at times and my being hard to handle. If you can't handle me at my worst though, then you sure as hell don't get my best...whaaat! "K.T.S.E.!" Especially those that allowed themselves to be "gassed up" by Autobots and the next individual's feelings and emotions. Yeah, I'm always inside of a moment. It's what I do when it comes to trials and tribulations. So, I don't avoid the inevitable. Do know though, it's always better to not "fit in" than to "fit into" a bunch of shit or shenanigans that you might not agree with or like.

    Saying that to say, always do and be you, no pressure! "Stay downs" or "lay downs," it's easy to lay down, it's hard as fuck to stay down, real talk, and that's why I ain't cool with niggahs, bitches, baby mamas and so-called family as I once was, balancing my "lows," how can you argue an outcome you can see? I'm vigilant about my balance and always trying to be in front of my consciousness, which is important to set an "intention." It makes for better captured moments, choosing this lifestyle we choose, being "street niggahs" and "real niggahs." For the bullshit niggahs, my shortest prayer in the world...fuck 'em!!! With coming to overstand, know and learn what it is to experience and be exposed to what it is I've aired out. For the most part they're survival mechanisms and tactics to navigate your way, a form of a guide, if you will.

    Survival mechanisms and tactics by way of a guide, to have a dude get focused, along with being aware of the many traps and pitfalls that's

## FEELING SOME TYPE OF WAY—SODO AUSTIN

out there waiting to have at a dude, by dudes pressing play on Autobotism, dirty politics and shenanigans (SMH), with many I had an all praise is due to Allah, to Allah we belong and to Him we return moments. That part of it is a given in the streets as being DP'ed and voted off the island in the maze. Fucking around, you're going to find yourself with and in many Mickey situations. Having many moments, some didn't realize what they were signing up for when they jumped in with both grey Chucks. Then coming to find out it gets very hot in the kitchen on the thirty-third, on some real life shit and on some real niggah shit.

Oh yeah, it gets Mickey and that mutha fucka gets hot, suuuper hot. Finding yourself in the thick of it, b'cuz shit goes from zero to a hot sixty. There's so many elements and no one's above being affected, being touched, or beyond being touched, it's always a "power" that be, a power unforseen and out of your control. At the end of the day, when it's a dude's time, it's his time. He's the fuck up out of there and quick like. That's just keeping it so one hunnid. A dude been politicked on and voted off of the island. Here we go again, another mama with a piece of her heart being broken from losing and grieving her son who'd been lost to the streets. The very streets she tried to warn him about, mama tried. She tried to tell him, b'cuz she knew couldn't nothing good come from being in them.

There's obstacles and challenges you're going to face...East Side! That's going to be present them self. Most of them are going to come disguised in the form of homie'ism, street'ism, turf'ism, Autobotism, political'ism (street and maze politics) and real niggah'ism. The other obstacles and elements that are having play pressed are just a part of what

## FEELING SOME TYPE OF WAY—SODO AUSTIN

comes with the lifestyle and a dude's daily existence above ground. I mean, shit, life is just funny that way. As with shit that comes imminent once you put yourself on the field of play. Putting yourself in certain types of situations, that took on a life of its own. "The maze ain't ever full and the Reaper ain't ever biased!" The imminent inevitable, it becomes a dude's existence. Overstand too though, at some point we have to check ourselves and slow our roll, b'cuz we can be doing way too much and not really realizing how we're pushing is basically counterproductive.

    Counterproductiveness draws unwanted attention to our push, from haters, Autobots, snitches, homies, the Ones and from IDK's looking from a distance ands lurking like a shadow niggah. That's unnecessary energy being fed to a mutha fucka that lives off being fed energy to survive, to be a means to an end or appear bigger than they are, or appearing to be gang gang. When the reality is, it's just faces of the different orchestrators and conductors of the bullshit. In the life we lead as jackers, bangers, gang members, street niggahs and rabb getting niggahs, there's a bigger captured moment and bigger than us. There's always a dude just as passionate as you, if not more. Do know a more passionate niggah is a more motivated niggah.

    We can't get too caught up with or in the trivial. Or thinking too much about the wrong shit, or getting in our own heads. Anything with the results of other dudes thinking. They definitely think too much about the wrong shit and you'll be sagging it out behind a crafty politician, pushing his crafty politics. You would've thought, though, niggahs like that

## FEELING SOME TYPE OF WAY—SODO AUSTIN

would've learned from the "boomerang gang," what goes around comes around. Yet so caught up in their ways, all they know is Mickey shit, shenanigans and craftiness, being an orchestrator of all things bullshit! They can't see beyond that until they're forced to, forced to see it. Yeah, the streets are funny that way too. No dude is above being touched or beyond being touched, and to think that he's pushing with a false sense of security...horseplaying! That's me calling a ball a ball and a strike a strike.

Clearly a bad look and a mis-overstanding, a dude is clearly and highly delusional, I can bang that. Moving along, none of what was said in these chapters that shaped and formed "Feeling Some Type Of Way," giving it its foundation weren't exclusive, the pains or trauma weren't exclusive. The different feelings and emotions causing you to feel some type of way wasn't exclusive. The weariness, the hater'ism, the snitching, the Mickey situations, none of those were exclusive. As with being bagged, banged or wrapped up. You're knowing this, you have to always be mindful of your elements and your surroundings. Especially who you're dealing with, everyone isn't who they portray to be. Take nothing or anyone for granted, at all. Our lifestyles are being took for granted based on. It's just a bad look, nothing good comes from it.

Get your mind around it and see it for what it and ain't, we already know what it is though, being an illusion. With that being said, I guess I'll park this pen momentarily, and I'm "back to it" (writing). I'm about to jump into "a Bitterchild state of mind." Can't stop, don't stop, won't stop! A'ight, y'all keep it above ground and be safe in this bullshit world as we

## FEELING SOME TYPE OF WAY—SODO AUSTIN

know it to be. K.T.S.E , always. It's not us that has us "pressured up," it's them...East Side!

    Any type of move/niggahs roll the dice/big uppin lil niggahs/read the kite/dirty vermin played it smoove/never closed his eyes/Autobots in transition/shit's bound to fly/lil Tic got it crackin/no disguise/chopped it up with field niggahs/yeah the code of silence/straight loyal to the soil/don't have to think about it/homies on the East/can't move without it/just a gang gang Crip/cuz dip through the crowd/yard bum status homie/eyes of the falcon/cock the hammer on the banger niggah/stretch you out/play pussy get fucked/got 'em screamin the loudest/fuckin wit 'em, duckin wit 'em/quick to get ouddied/a native of Long Beach/the whole gang get rowdy/known for gang sweeps/flocks and bounties/hit the maze/and a couple of stints in the county/keep it true blue/one hunnid/to the shit that bound me/sky's kind ah cloudy/a niggah tears in a bucket/the walk of a BG/pressin fa Long Beach/til I can't breathe/some claim that I'm extreme/cuz I'm tatted wit the East/fuck if you don't like me/you can see what I mean/a worst case of the fuck its/y'all know me/yeah you can trust it...

# FEELING SOME TYPE OF WAY—SODO AUSTIN

Look for projects coming up:
by Sodo Austin
"A Bitterchild State Of Mind"
and "Yard Life" (Exposé, Real Life Inside Of Prison) - II

www.ingramcontent.com/pod-product-compliance
Lightning Source LLC
Chambersburg PA
CBHW052137070526
44585CB00017B/1861